ACQ 6060

Writing
as a Way of Knowing

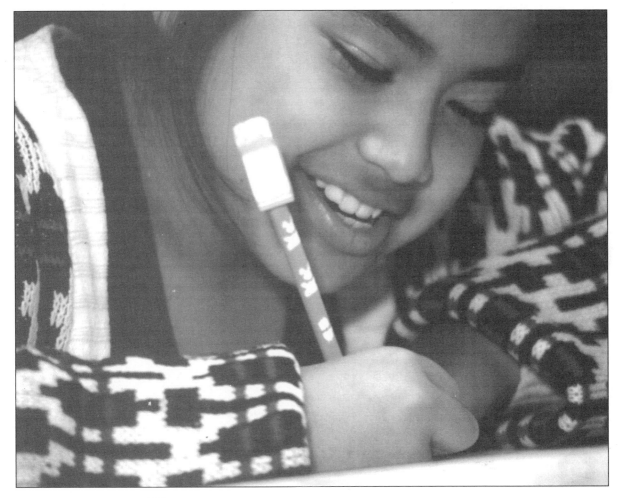

LOIS BRIDGES

Stenhouse Publishers

The Galef Institute

Strategies for Teaching and Learning Professional Library

Administrators: Supporting School Change by Robert Wortman
Assessment: Continuous Learning by Lois Bridges
Creating Your Classroom Community by Lois Bridges
Dance as a Way of Knowing by Jennifer Zakkai
Drama as a Way of Knowing by Paul G. Heller
Literature as a Way of Knowing by Kathy G. Short
Math as a Way of Knowing by Susan Ohanian
Music as a Way of Knowing by Nick Page
Second Language Learners by Stephen Cary
Writing as a Way of Knowing by Lois Bridges

Look for announcements of future titles in this series on science and visual arts.

Stenhouse Publishers, 431 York Street, York, Maine 03909
The Galef Institute, 11050 Santa Monica Boulevard, Third Floor, Los Angeles, California 90025

Library of Congress Cataloging-in-Publication Data
Bridges, Lois.
    Writing as a way of knowing / Lois Bridges.
        p.   cm.—(Strategies for teaching and learning professional library)
    Includes bibliographical references (p.   ).
    ISBN 1-571100-062-8 (alk. paper)
    1. English language—Composition and exercises—Study and teaching
    (Elementary)—United States. 2. Creative writing (Elementary
    education)—United States. I. Title. II. Series.
    LB1576.B4963 1997
    372.62'3'044—dc21   97-16320
                                                                     CIP

Manufactured in the United States of America on acid-free paper.
00   8 7 6 5 4 3

Dear Colleague,

The extraordinary resource books in this series support our common goal as educators to apply best practices to everyday teaching. These books will encourage you to examine new resources and to discover and try out new and different teaching strategies. We hope you'll want to discuss and reflect on your strategies with other teachers and coaches in your support study group meetings (both face-to-face and virtual) to make the most of the rich learning and teaching opportunities each discipline offers.

If we truly believe that all children can be successful in school, then we must find ways to help all children develop to their full potential. This requires an understanding of how children learn, thoughtful preparation of curriculum, continuous reflection, adaptation of everyday practices, and ongoing professional support. To that end, the *Strategies for Teaching and Learning Professional Library* was developed. The series offers you countless opportunities for professional growth. It's rather like having your own workshops, coaching, and study groups between the covers of a book.

Each book in this series invites you to explore
- the theory regarding human learning and development—so you know why,
- the best instructional practices—so you know how, and
- continuous assessment of your students' learning as well as your own teaching and understanding—so you and your students know that you know.

The books offer *Dialogues* to reflect upon your practices, on your own and in study groups. The Dialogues invite responses to self-evaluative questions, and encourage experimentation with new instructional strategies.

Shoptalks provide short, lively reviews of the best and latest professional literature as well as professional journals and associations.

Teacher-To-Teacher Field Notes are full of tips and experiences from other practicing educators who offer different ways of thinking about teaching practices and a wide range of successful, practical classroom strategies and techniques to draw upon.

It's our hope that as you explore and reflect on your teaching practice, you'll continue to expand your teaching repertoire and share your success with your colleagues.

Sincerely,

Linda Adelman-Johannesen

Linda Adelman-Johannesen
President
The Galef Institute

The Strategies for Teaching and Learning Professional Library is part of the Galef Institute's school reform initiative *Different Ways of Knowing*.

Different Ways of Knowing is a philosophy of education based on research in child development, cognitive theory, and multiple intelligences. It offers teachers, administrators, artists and other specialists, and other school and district educators continuing professional growth opportunities integrated with teaching and learning materials. The materials are supportive of culturally and linguistically diverse school populations and help all teachers and children to be successful. Teaching strategies focus on interdisciplinary, thematic instruction integrating history and social studies with the performing and visual arts, literature, writing, math, and science. Developed with the leadership of Senior Author Linda Adelman-Johannesen, *Different Ways of Knowing* has been field tested in hundreds of classrooms across the country.

For more information, contact

The Galef Institute
11050 Santa Monica Boulevard, Third Floor, Los Angeles, California 90025
Tel 310.479.8883
Fax 310.473.9720
www.dwoknet.galef.org

Strategies for Teaching and Learning Professional Library

Contributors

President
Linda Adelman-Johannesen

Senior Vice President
Sue Beauregard

Editors
Resa Gabe Nikol
Susan Zinner

Editorial Assistant
Elizabeth Finison

Designer
Delfina Marquez-Noé

Photographers
Ted Beauregard
Dana Ross

I am grateful to the many teachers who have taught me about writing: my professional mentors, Nancie Atwell, Lucy Calkins, Ralph Fletcher, Shelley Harwayne, Donald Murray, and Brenda Ueland. A heartfelt thank you to Donald Graves whose passion for writing and generosity of spirit continue to inspire millions of teachers and their students. I thank my teacher mentors, Greg Chapnick, Debi Goodman, and Rena Malkofsky, as well as the teachers from the National Writing Project who so generously shared their writing stories and insights: Pam Bovyer Cook, Marie Therese Janise, Laura Schwartzberg, and Sherry Swain. And a special thank you to my personal mentors: my dear children, Aislinn, Erin, and Brennan who delight me daily with their own literate insights; and my beloved parents, Alice Bridges, artist and poet, and father, Hal Bridges, the most talented writer I know whose loving, expert writing lessons over the years guide every sentence I write.   —LB

Special thanks to Andrew G. Galef and Bronya Pereira Galef for their continuing commitment to our nation's children and educators.

Contents

Chapter 1
Why Write?

Writing, like reading and arithmetic, is supposed to be taught in school. Children are supposed to learn how to write. But beyond the conventional wisdom that knowing how to write is important, how often do we really consider what writing is for?

My youngest daughter, Erin, is eleven now, but when she was six she taught me an important lesson about the purpose of writing.

I was editing a book on assessment, working almost daily, with a 6 pm deadline for overnight mail. That meant that by 4 pm, I was keeping my eye on the clock, carefully gauging how much more work I could complete before I had to make my mail dash.

One day, soon after the new school year had started, I was frantically trying to meet my daily deadline when Erin burst through the front door with her best friend, Becca. "Mommmm, hurry! Come here, quick! There's a baby bird and it's dead! And ants are on it! You've got to come!"

I groaned silently to myself. The last thing I wanted to deal with was a dead baby bird, particularly one that was being devoured by ants. But performing my maternal duty, I rose reluctantly from my desk and went to meet the anxious girls who were waiting by the front door.

"Hurry, Momma!" Erin grabbed my hand and pulled me through the front door.

She led me to the edge of our front lawn and sure enough, what had once been a living, heart-beating baby sparrow was now a tiny corpse.

"Oh, girls, there's nothing we can do. The bird might be diseased. Let's leave the poor thing alone." Enough said and done, I hurried back inside to finish my last bit of work.

Back at my desk, I became vaguely aware of the comings and goings of the girls. I saw them out in the backyard, searching through the tool shed and emerging with a garden trowel and spade. I heard them in the kitchen, rummaging around in the junk drawer and whispering about tape and string. But I had my mission—to meet my deadline, so I paid them little mind.

Finally, with minutes to spare, I grabbed the pouch, jammed in the manuscript and disk, and raced for the front door. I swung open the door, and nearly fell over my daughter and her friend who were kneeling near the flower beds just outside the house.

We write to find meaning, to make sense, to record events that matter.

There, amongst the white impatiens, was a small, oval mound outlined with smooth, white pebbles ("borrowed" from our next door neighbors' graveled yard). "See, Mom," Erin pointed to the mound, "we buried the bird."

At the head of the tiny grave was a wooden cross, fashioned from two twigs secured with a shoelace. But what made me catch my breath was a note the girls had written and taped to the cross.

When we buried this bird we were sad. We wondered for a long time how the bird died.

"We had to let everyone know how we felt," Erin explained. I realized, with a pang, that Erin and Becca had been grappling with the mysteries of life and death. While I, in my rushed adult world, had dismissed the dead sparrow as something of a nuisance, they had been profoundly affected by the discovery of its crumpled body. Trying to make sense of it all, they had turned to writing. Writing helped them explain to the world that this little bird had lived, it had mattered, and they had been saddened by its death.

Doesn't Erin's and Becca's experience crystallize the reasons why we write? We write to find meaning, to make sense, to record events that matter.

S H O P T A L K

Calkins, Lucy McCormick with Shelley Harwayne. *Living Between the Lines*. Portsmouth, New Hampshire: Heinemann, 1991.

Writing and literacy are not and should not be separate from living, Calkins maintains. But how do we help our students live their writing, to care about it as passionately as they might a school soccer game or a sleepover at a friend's house? Calkins shows us how writing notebooks, the ubiquitous writer's tool, can bring life and literacy together in ways that matter to all students. Instead of keeping writing folders stuffed with separate pieces, Calkins suggests that teachers and students do as professional writers do: Use a notebook—spiral, marbled composition, looseleaf, or bound—as a place to gather ideas, let them germinate, revisit them, play with them, and wait to see if one might push through and blossom. Additionally, she shows teachers how to use writing notebooks to move children into engaging learning projects, alternative genres, and how to weave literature throughout.

Writing Is Lifework

"Writing is *lifework*, not desk work," writes Lucy Calkins, the author of four important books on children and teachers and writing. In *Living Between the Lines* (1991), she reminds us that "literacy and life are not, and should not be separate. Writing and reasons to write are all around us"—the premature death of a baby sparrow, a new haircut that's five inches shorter than what you had wanted, an embarrassing moment at the grocery checkout stand when the clerk rings up your bill and you've just discovered that you've left your wallet at home. It is from these incidents, from the rich material of our own lives, that we can draw upon for our writing.

As Calkins explains, real writing is meant to "unfold and stretch into every aspect of the writer's world." Writing helps us "live wide-awake lives," to notice, to pay tribute to, and to remember the small details of our lives that too often simply pass through our consciousness. Life is an unremitting flow of events. As my daughter Erin has discovered through her journals, writing not only helps us stop and capture life's moments, it also helps us give shape to our daily experiences and to make sense of things that are happening to us.

Writing is not just about preserving and understanding personal experience; writing serves many purposes. In school, as in life, writing is also very much about expanding personal learning horizons and being able to show others what you've learned about science, history, math, geography, and astronomy. Writing is an entryway into all our marvelous human knowledge and information.

In general, however, it's easier to learn about writing itself, and to play with its many subtle and complex intricacies, when we are writing on the comfortable territory of our own personal experience—about things that matter to us and that we know well. This is as true for adults as it is for children.

Claim the Wide World of Writing

Using language is much like being a fish in water—language swirls through us and around us almost continuously. We're seldom conscious of its many purposes. So, to make written language manifest, try this exercise. Keep track of everything you read or write for twenty-four hours. Sounds simple, doesn't it? Well, we'll see what you think after you've tried this activity. Take a notebook with you in the car, to the supermarket, in every room of your home—yes, everywhere.

So, what did you find out? Truly, language serves myriad roles and performs multiple functions! If you were true to the exercise and dutifully recorded everything you read for a twenty-four hour period (and it's almost impossible to do; our environment virtually drips with print), you probably encountered and interacted with written language that

- informs
- warns
- describes
- delights
- persuades
- dissuades
- inspires
- hires
- and?

Field Notes: Teacher-To-Teacher

Early in the year, my second and third graders brainstorm a list of all the ways in which people use writing. They are surprised to see the size of the list and that there are so many reasons for writing other than to create stories. For homework, I also have children interview their parents to find out how they use writing at home and at work. Children love doing interviews, and this is an effective way to involve parents in what their children are doing in school. We share the information that they gathered and add any new ideas to the list that they have generated in school.

Laura Schwartzberg
P.S. 234
New York, New York

Now, think about your writing program. Are your students experiencing the full spectrum of literacy? Do they have opportunities to jot down lists, create poems, compose plays or songs, design advertisements, record learning reflections, and so on?

Don't be embarrassed or feel bad if you're forced to admit "no." Writing in American schools has focused almost exclusively on expository writing (book reports, answers to end-of-the-chapter questions, teacher-assigned research reports) with an occasional creative writing experience in response to language arts guidelines. For the most part, we American educators have never understood writing nor felt particularly comfortable with it. So how can you expand the writing possibilities in your classroom and help your students discover all the marvelous things that writing can do? How can you help them claim the wide world of writing?

Sixth-grade teacher Toby Curry, at the Dewey Center for Urban Education in Detroit, offers some good advice. "There are regular, ongoing writing invitations in my class, but I still keep a posted list of twenty-five writing project possibilities that I share each fall with kids and parents. This list stays on the wall all year. I never hear, 'I don't have anything to do,' mainly because our ideas for writing are always producing more new ideas for writing."

Read to Children—Share the Writing Possibilities

It takes time to discover all that writing can do. Perhaps the best way to learn is to read. Author Gary Paulson tells young writers, "Read like a wolf eats" (quoted in Fletcher 1993).

But, if you've ever had the chance to read the autobiography of a well-known writer, then you know that there's something even better than silently devouring books. It's having someone you are close to read aloud to you and then talk about the reading, share their thoughts and feelings about the selection, point out particularly sparkling passages, and invite you to do the same. It's the thoughtful dialogue about reading that seems to make the critical difference in how we develop as writers. And not surprisingly, many famous authors share fond memories of being cradled in the lap of someone they loved while listening to and talking about a story, poem, or essay.

It takes time to discover all that writing can do.

Listen to what author Mem Fox (1993) says about being read to:

> From my own experience I realize that the literature I *heard*, rather than read, as a child resonates again and again in my memory whenever I sit down to write. It's the sounds I remember rather than the sight of words. Of course silent reading also fills our storehouses, but it is an immediate treat to be read aloud to, especially when the reader reads in a lively manner, enthusiastically, using his or her voice expressively to paint vivid pictures in our imaginations.

The human voice brings us not only the vocabulary and structure of powerful writing, but the music and rhythm as well. Furthermore, we begin to learn about all the possibilities of writing—all the many things writing can do and accomplish.

Sherry Swain, first-grade teacher at Overstreet Elementary School in Starkville, Mississippi, strives to make these writing possibilities visible and accessible for her students. For example, after reading *Wiley and the Hairy Man* by Molly Bang, her students examine the page where the Hairy Man is described. Swain explains, "I say to my students, Molly Bang could have simply said, 'The Hairy Man sure was ugly' and stopped. Instead, she tells us that he is hairy all over, that his eyes burned like coals, that his teeth were long and sharp and white. Which sounds more interesting? Why?" Swain maintains that the discussions that follow these mini-lessons on style allow the children to discover the power of detail in description.

For this reason, Shirley Brice Heath (1986) suggests that all it may take for children to grow into full literacy is a relationship with one adult who demonstrates what it means to be "joyfully literate": someone who shares with the child his or her love of language in all its varied manifestations;

someone who reads aloud and discusses the reading; and someone who asks real questions and isn't afraid to admit, "I don't know the answer to that question. How do you suppose we could find out?" So, as a critical first step in helping your young writers understand what writing is all about, read aloud to them—four, five, six times a day—whenever you have a spare moment. In my classroom, I made it a practice to keep at least one children's poetry anthology on my desk, ready to slip into those spontaneous "literary moments"—to fill the minutes before the lunch bell, to help transition into a new learning experience, to calm nerves during standardized testing time. And, of course, beyond the spontaneous moments you find for read-alouds, you'll want to create a ritualized time each day where you gather as a class and slip into the sacredness and intimacy of a shared reading experience.

Alicia Rivera teaches second grade at Hillcrest School in Oakland, California. She is a great lover of literature. Her classroom, lined with bookshelves, is filled with hundreds of books. She reads aloud an array of genres to her students—fairy tales, folktales, fables, short stories, picture books, poetry, and novels. Rivera explains, "From the start, and ever after, children need stories that will touch their hearts, tickle their funny bones, and challenge their intellects; stories that will ignite their imaginations and fashion their dreams. Children and teachers need classrooms filled with beautiful, wonderful books." Her students soon absorb Rivera's love of books and the magic that comes with it, as illustrated by the letter on page 14 she received from two of her former students who are now in third grade.

Children and teachers need classrooms filled with beautiful, wonderful books.

Dear Miss Rivera,
    Guess who we saw outside in
Discovery Center. We saw the
Emperor in the parade! A little
girl was saying that he had
no clothes on. Then we went
to the bathroom and saw
a miniature little Mermad in the sink.
Then we saw her godown the drain.
Then we saw the Princess of the School
door. The sun was shining bright and
she was driping wet. And there were peas
scattered in front of the 1Office.
And there were 20 Mattreses and
Fether Beds stacked on the bed in
the Nurses Room. Oh, and we forgot
to tell you ..... Peter Rabits (+ him)
send there love.
            From us..
            (and Betrix Pitter + Hans
            Christian Anderson and all the
            charecters from both of them.)

Marie Therese Janise, who teaches third grade at Richard Elementary
School in Acadia Parish, Louisiana, is also a passionate believer in the
power of literature to move children as writers. Janise writes, "I read to
my students several times a day, but, by far, our favorite time of the day
is when we gather together in a cozy corner of our classroom for shared
reading. We read the same book, poem, or song for an entire week. For
example, we may read *Millicent and the Wind* by Robert Munsch, *Wind
Song* by Lilian Moore, or sing "Weather the Storm" by Sarah Pirtle.
During the week we predict, infer, and discuss the author's style, use of
vocabulary, and other characteristics of the piece. We read together, listen to one another read, and act out our poems, thoroughly enjoying
literature."

What To Read Aloud
Review the list you created as you tried to keep track of your daily print
encounters. Most likely, you very quickly discovered that writing serves
many different purposes. Writing is not just about writing stories or research reports or poetry. We want children to know what all the writing
possibilities are—all the many uses writing has, all the many genres writing can assume. Help them claim the wide world of writing.

DIALOGUE

What are my memories of being read to? What was the first book I remember reading or having read to me?

_____

_____

How often do I read aloud to my students? Why do I read to them?

_____

_____

How can I increase read-aloud time?

_____

_____

What are my favorite read-alouds? Who are my favorite authors? Why? Who are my favorite illustrators? Why?

_____

_____

How might I expand my reading repertoire?

_____

_____

In addition to a collection of fine literature and poetry, for reading aloud, I recommend that you begin to collect effective written material of all kinds:

- persuasive letters to the editor
- catchy advertisements
- eyewitness news reports
- thought-provoking interviews
- provocative political essays
- song lyrics
- humorous memos

- colorful cookbook recipes
- easy-to-follow manuals
- heart-stopping sports accounts.

You get the idea. Writing can perform many roles. We want our students to slip into all those writing roles and wear them comfortably, to move from a letter to a pen-pal to a poem celebrating the birth of a baby sister as easily as they move from playground banter to polite conversation with the school principal. We want our students to control writing in all its many forms and functions, to be as fluid and flexible with written language as they are with oral language, to dance lightly across the wide world of writing.

Writing can perform many roles.

SHOPTALK

Harwayne, Shelley. *Lasting Impressions: Weaving Literature into the Writing Workshop*. Portsmouth, New Hampshire: Heinemann, 1992.

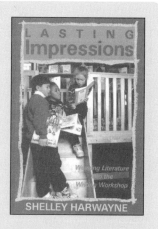

"Shelley Harwayne uses her book to explore the question, 'How does the literature we read inform the literature we write?' This is an excellent, practical book for teachers who are just beginning to try implementing a writing workshop," writes third grade teacher, Marie Therese Janise, "and for those who may wish to re-examine their practices. The book is divided into two parts. The first part shows how to use literature to develop a community among readers and writers at the beginning of the school year. The second part shows how this newly developed community can work together to become critical readers and writers. Harwayne covers such topics as conferencing, mini-lessons, reading response groups, and genres."

For teachers and parents who want recommendations for quality literature, Janise recommends these guides:

Lipson, Eden Ross. *The New York Times Parent's Guide to the Best Books for Children*. New York: Times Books, 1988.

Stott, Jon C. *Children's Literature from A to Z: A Guide for Parents and Teachers*. New York: McGraw-Hill Book Company, 1984.

Trelease, Jim. *The Read-Aloud Handbook*. New York: Penguin, 1995.

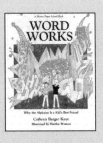
Take a Language Bath

Visualize holding a baby in your arms and immersing that baby in warm bath water. Watch the baby smile as the warm water washes over the baby's body.

With that image in your mind, switch your visual picture to your classroom. Visualize your students immersed in written language—print of all sorts surrounds them, filling their ears and eyes with soothing, amusing, informing, performing, rich, wonderful language! There are many ways to immerse your students in language. For starters, here are three suggestions:

1. Read aloud all sorts of material as frequently as possible. Talk about what you are reading and discuss what makes it effective.

   Linda Buchanan, a Media Specialist at Church Street Elementary School in Tupelo, Mississippi, finds that storytelling is a powerful way to help children love stories. Buchanan writes, "One of my students said, 'You know when you read to us, it's a good story, but when you tell it, it's like it really happened.'"

2. Cover your classroom walls with print (and invite students to do the same). Refer to the print frequently and change it often to include

   - announcements
   - messages
   - directions
   - editorials
   - recipes
   - poetry
   - schedules
   - quotable quotes
   - advertisements
   - cartoons
   - labels
   - signs
   - song banners
   - classroom correspondence
   - news articles
   - student projects.

Pam Bovyer Cook, a fifth-sixth grade teacher in Oakland, California, reminds us that reading and writing are "embedded in the flow of daily life." Bovyer Cook finds, especially for her inner city students, that it's important to showcase this environmental print to help students understand that literacy is useful and serves a great many purposes. Following the lead of Yetta Goodman and Bess Attwerger (1981), she recommends taking students on a literacy walk of their neighborhood, pointing out such environmental print as street signs, billboards, and store-front ads.

3. Invite kids to find their own real reasons to write, and establish time to share, discuss, and celebrate all the different kinds of writing that your students are exploring.

Toby Curry, who teaches sixth grade in Detroit, informs me that one of her colleagues actually bolted a refrigerator door to her classroom wall to showcase all the wide-ranging print such doors often display.

DIALOGUE

What kinds of printed material are evident in my classroom? What purposes do they serve?

_____

_____

_____

What kinds of different genres and writing functions have my students explored?

_____

_____

_____

How can I expand the writing world in my classroom?

_____

_____

_____

Field Notes: Teacher-To-Teacher

To develop literacy, the most important activity I provide is ample opportunity to read and write. I tell my students it's like learning to ride a bicycle. You can't learn how to ride just by staring at the bike or even by reading about it. You have to get on, fall off, get back up, fall again, and again, and again. Eventually, you will start riding without falling too many times. After more practice, you will begin to ride a little more smoothly. Later on you will ride even better. You may even learn to do some tricks and break a few rules. If you practice a whole lot, you may even get to be as competitive as a bicycle racer. It's exactly the same with language. You have to read and write in order to read and write. The more you practice, the better you get.

Greg Chapnick
Charquin School
Hayward, California

When we care about our writing, we're more likely to invest the time and energy that makes for vital writing.

Lessons from Young Writers

Perhaps the best way to share the possibilities of writing is to pull from my file drawer and share with you the wide range of children's writing I've collected over the years, and invite you to think about what these examples might mean for your writing program. You'll notice that these samples are written by children of all ages. Children as young as five can use writing to serve many purposes.

These writing samples offer vibrant examples of kids writing to serve their own purposes. These are not assigned writing pieces. These young authors wrote with the freedom of choice and control. Mem Fox suggests that when we use writing to serve our own purposes—whatever those purposes might be—we're much more likely to really care about our writing. Indeed, she says our goal as writing teachers is to help our students "ache with caring" over their chosen topics. When we care about our writing, we're more likely to invest the time and energy that makes for vital writing. I'm reminded of the *Velveteen Rabbit* by Margery Williams Bianco, the stuffed toy rabbit who became "real" only after it had been loved and cared for by its youthful owner.

Our students' writing will come to life when they love what they are writing and care about it passionately because it's helping them accomplish something they want to do. Why write? There are as many reasons to write as there are individuals in the world. Writing can be both intensely personal and uniquely public. Here are some writing examples from students, ages five to eleven, who show us the living possibilities of writing. Come tour the wide world of writing. (How many different genres do you see?)

Paleontologist Tells All

A first-grade paleontologist? Why not? He knows his dinosaurs and he knows how to help others know—and care about—what he knows.

ALASAUrUS WAS A
MEATe EATere iT
AET ATHr DiNASAUrS
Like For iNStiNS
hi hAD NO TrOBL
AT ALL WEN hi ATAcD
A BABY BRONTOSAUrUS
iT WAS ESE PrAE For
him TYRONNOSAUrUS ReX
WASThe KeNg OF
DiNOSSAUeS iT AET
ALASAUrUS SoM TimeS

Alosaurus was a meat eater. It ate other dinosaurs. Like, for instance, he had no trouble at all when he attacked a baby *Brontosaurus*. It was easy prey for him. *Tyrannosaurus rex* was the king of dinosaurs. It ate *Alosaurus* sometimes.

The Organized Life

Not one to trust the important details of daily living to happenstance, Lauren Montgomery, age five, devoted every evening for two weeks to composing a list to guide her through the next day. One of her lists is on page 21.

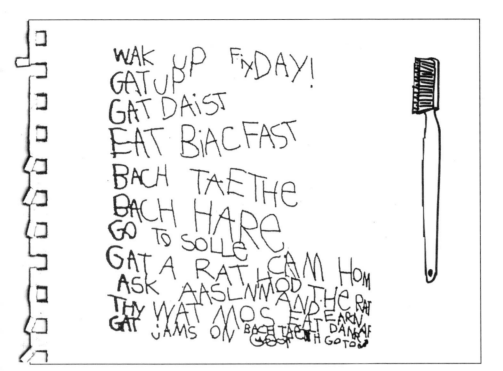

Wake up Friday! Get up Get dressed Eat breakfast Brush teeth Brush hair Go to school Come home Get a rat Hold the rat Ask Aislinn and Erin if they want Mousey Eat dinner Get jammies on Brush teeth Go to bed

Poem for the Homeland
Hang Nguyen lives in Portland, Oregon, and was eleven years old when he wrote this poem.

Spring

Every morning of spring, when the sun is coming up,
a crowd of flowers bloom,
opening their pretty eyes.
Birds are singing.
All carry me to my dear country.
Remembering all the things I miss.
What a beautiful morning!
And all the garden is filled with long green grass
and roses and flowers.
Flowers are a gift of love for friends.
They are the background of love.
But sometimes they carry a heart broken,
a reminder of a lost land.

From *Treasures 2: Stories and Art by Students in Oregon* © 1988 edited by Chris Weber

Clunker Bike

Seven-year-old Bennet had repeatedly asked his parents for a new bicycle, but had been denied. As a last resort, he asked his "Clunker Bike" to write a note on his behalf.

> Kick me hit Me throw me away
> I can't out run a garden slug
> My chain fell off I 10 I'm older then Ben
> my paints peeling I'm rusty I'm missing bolts
> and screw ether get and by Benanewbike Ormake
> him inbarressa when ever He rides Me.
>   Sighned, Clunker bike

Kick me, hit me, throw me away. I can't out run a garden slug. My chain fell off. I'm 10; I'm older than Ben. My paint's peeling. I'm rusty. I'm missing bolts and screws. Either get and buy Ben a new bike, or make him embarrassed whenever he rides me. Signed, Clunker Bike.

Calendar of Life

The students in Pine Gulch School in Bolinas, California, spent a year studying their local natural environment. They celebrated their knowledge and raised money for their school at the same time by putting together a beautiful calendar. Their lovely sketches graced each month. Here are their drawings for the month of June.

Division Was Never This Much Fun

The students in Margaret Klemenkoff's fifth-grade class at Orion School in Redwood City, California, keep learning logs for all subjects, including math. In the logs, Margaret asks them to write about their evolving understanding of the subject. Michael found a way to make division a lot more fun than I ever remember it being.

LIGHT SPEED⟫⟫⟫
goes to Division land!

I, Light Speed, the fastest dude this side of the dimensional spectrum, decided to take a vacation to bermuda, triangle that is! So I headed down there and when I got there I took a closer look and all of a sudden a green beam hit me and pulled me in On the other side was Division Land. they attacked but I flew of at all 186,282 mps but they hit me with a division ray that devided my speed by 2, reducing my speed to 93,141 mps. But I still strived, but they hit me with another ray and I shrunk, they devided my height of 6 feet by 3 and then I was 2 feet tall. I got away just barely. I came upon a boy named 1 who was obviously a lower number who had been devided into a lower number He said he wanted me to multiply him by 20, so I did and he became a big muscular guy named 20. And we whent and saw the queen next. I got a division gun and blasted her and devided her by 11 into from a 99 by 9 into an 11. than 20 devided the queen a 1 and 20 became the good King 20 of Division Land and I got all of my powers back and left. The End

Reflect To Learn

Students can use writing to reflect on their learning—to take stock of what's working for them and to assess what might not be working as well. This Tucson, Arizona, student reflects on her learning life in second grade and, overall, is pleased with her development.

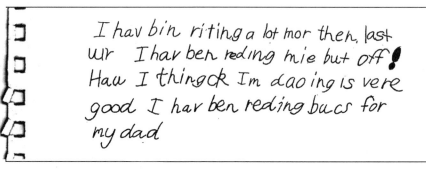

These young writers know how to make writing work for them. Why not start a "What's Writing For?" display in your classroom and invite your students to bring in writing they do at home, at school, in Bob's Donut Shop, in the car—wherever! Together, you'll discover and come to appreciate exactly what writing is for—just about anything!

Fifth-grade writer Heidi Bimschleger knows why she writes. "I have found another side of myself that I've never known before. When I leave fifth grade, I'm not going to stop writing because I don't want to close up a world that I just unlocked."

Chapter 2
Discover Your Writing Self

I'm the teacher. Why do I have to write? That's the question I muttered to myself on my first day as a participant in the Southern Arizona Writing Project as the instructor explained that we would spend most of our time writing. And that may be the question you are asking right now. We're going to write because it's very difficult to be an effective teacher of writing if you haven't, to some extent, experienced writing yourself. Like anything else, it's very hard to teach something that you don't do.

For example, we laugh at the absurdity of sending a child to learn piano from a piano teacher who doesn't play the piano and doesn't even own a piano. But we routinely send children to teachers who don't write, never write, and don't own a writing notebook or computer.

Perhaps that's because we think that writing is magical, handed down from the heavens to only a gifted few. But it's not. Writing is for everyone. Anyone can learn to write. But it won't happen without practice. Just like everything else, if we want to learn how to write, we have to practice writing the same way we practice cooking, or cross-country skiing, or gardening, or ballroom dancing. We have to use our writing muscles or they'll get flabby.

The first thing we'll do is think about our own relationship to writing. Over the years, I've come to feel reasonably comfortable with myself as a writer, although it wasn't always that way. My breakthrough came in 1978 when I participated in the first Southern Arizona Writing Project (SAWP), a regional project spawned by the Bay Area Writing Project. Nearly two decades later, there are now numerous regional projects that function under the leadership of the National Writing Project. These Writing Projects bring teachers together to learn about writing through their own writing.

I didn't understand that I'd actually have to write when, following the recommendation of University of Arizona Professor Yetta Goodman, I was invited to participate in SAWP. I taught first grade on the Tohono O'odham Reservation, about seventy-five miles southwest of Tucson, Arizona. I had always invited my first graders to write in whatever way they could—even though, at that time in the 70s, many teachers delayed writing until third grade when children could control the conventions of writing—spelling, punctuation, and so on. I wanted to learn more about how to help my first graders as writers. I certainly didn't think that meant helping *myself* as a writer!

As soon as the SAWP instructor explained our daily schedule for the eight weeks we would spend together, I wanted to bolt for the door. He explained that we'd spend the morning writing about whatever we wanted. During lunch, our writing from the morning would be typed up, mimeographed, and everyone would receive a copy. We would spend the afternoons in small groups, discussing and responding to our colleagues' writing. I panicked. I was the only elementary school teacher in a room of high school English teachers and college freshman English instructors. They all wrote themselves. They taught writing. They seemed to consider themselves writers. I didn't write. I didn't really teach writing to my first graders. And I most certainly was not a writer.

Why I stayed, I'll never know—perhaps I felt it would be embarrassing to drop out after Dr. Goodman had recommended me. At any rate, I'm so grateful that I stuck it out. Once I got past my terror, I discovered my voice as a writer through the daily act of writing. I found out that I did have something to say and I began to play with different ways of saying it.

What Professional Writers Do

My participation in SAWP also gave me a glimpse into the world of professional writers. Through my own writing—and the complete freedom we had in SAWP to write about whatever we wanted—I began to understand how professional writing evolves. Professional writers (as distinguished from school writers) control their own writing from start to finish. Professional writers

- choose their own writing topics
- decide their own purposes for writing
- target their own audiences

DIALOGUE

Take a moment now to consider your feelings about yourself as writer.

How do I feel about writing?

_____

_____

How often do I write?

_____

_____

Why do I write?

_____

_____

Do I consider myself a writer? Why or why not?

_____

_____

What would I change about myself as a writer?

_____

_____

- establish their own writing schedules
- share their writing with trusted peers
- draft and redraft
- publish their writing (if they're lucky!).

At first, I found the freedom of choice and control terrifying. But ultimately, as I began to discover my writing self, the freedom was both liberating and exhilarating. And I realized that without freedom of choice and control, it's probably not possible to reach the writing self. Choice and control are so basic to professional writing that, without them, I'm not sure our true

Writing is a magnet that draws thoughts and feelings and images and understandings to the bright surface of your paper.

writing selves can emerge. I did lots and lots of writing in school, but teachers almost always controlled my writing. They told me what to write, how to write it, when to write it, and they were my only audience. And their interest in reading my writing never stemmed much beyond giving me credit for completing their assignments and a letter grade for the Language Arts space on my report card.

No wonder school writing was so laborious. Ignoring it until the night before it was due, I completed it under the abject fear of not getting a passing grade.

My school writing self bore no resemblance to the writing self that emerged during the eight weeks I spent in SAWP. And, not surprisingly, my writing in SAWP bore no resemblance to the writing I had done in school. I began to play with different genres, poetry in particular. I wrote my autobiography in a straight chronological order and then, inspired by discussions with my colleagues, I rewrote it beginning with a flashback from my high school days. I experimented. I took risks. I felt free to drop a piece if it wasn't working. And, for the first time, I discovered the value and satisfaction of revision. Before then, I had related revision to punishment for not getting it right the first time.

And I made the most amazing discovery of all—writing itself is discovery. Writing is a magnet that draws thoughts and feelings and images and understandings to the bright surface of your paper. Sometimes, you actually discover what you are going to say in the process of writing it. What an astonishing discovery! School had led me to believe that writing meant doing all your thinking beforehand and simply transcribing that mental text onto paper. Imagine—writing to think; writing to *discover* what you know and what you want to say.

And, while sharing my writing with my SAWP colleagues was initially one of the scariest things I've ever done, by the second week I found that I was craving their response, and was terribly disappointed if our sharing time ended before I'd had a chance to share my writing.

These were the understandings that I carried back to my first-grade class in the fall. Once I knew myself as a writer and understood the importance of choice and control, I understood how to help my students discover their writing selves. Let's explore these understandings now, focusing on topic choice first.

What To Write About

> Everyone is talented, original, and has something important to say.
>
> –Brenda Ueland, 1938

Carl Sandburg called Brenda Ueland, author and writing teacher, the greatest teacher of writing that ever lived. So, the greatest teacher of writing (in Carl Sandburg's opinion) believed, with all her heart, that every student who came to her—and people from all walks of life sought her help: milkmen, secretaries, lawyers, actors, store clerks, gardeners—had interesting and unique things to say, drawn from the original material of their own lives.

As I work with my students, I try very hard to keep Ueland's words in mind. I want to believe in every student, as Ueland did. Of course, it's easy to receive Tamara's writing knowing that within the context of a terrific plot, I'll find a delightful turn of phrase or a particularly striking character description. It's not as easy to believe Ueland when I work with students who struggle just to get a sentence or two down on paper. But Ueland said everyone.

It was Roberto who helped me believe Ueland. Roberto spent his days in class slumped back in his desk, legs sprawled straight out, arms resting on his belly. While other children traversed the room, chatting with friends, gathering supplies to complete their work, it seemed that Roberto's primary goal was not to alter his position.

But one day, after another topic launch in our writer's workshop in which I simply said, "Write about something you know a lot about," Roberto rather quickly produced an eight-page essay detailing his knowledge of rabbits. It turned out that Roberto had kept rabbits for several years and knew everything about how to care for them, their habits, their social relationships, how

Once I knew myself as a writer and understood the importance of choice and control, I understood how to help my students discover their writing selves.

they reproduced and cared for their young. As I read his paper, I realized with delight that I was learning from Roberto. He was teaching me the important, original stuff he knew about rabbits. Ueland was right.

Ueland was right because she knew something critically important about writing topics. She knew that it's much easier to write about something you know a lot about or care a lot about; it's not at all easy to write about things you don't know. Even professional writers wouldn't attempt that. They immerse themselves in research about a topic and spend days reading about, thinking about, and talking to experts about their chosen topic. Only after days of studying and reflecting on the topic are they ready to begin writing.

If we want our students to write interesting and original material, we have to invite them to write about topics they really care about. It's just simply true that it's much easier to write about things that matter to you.

Teachers often say, "But my kids can't think of their own topics. Assigning a topic gives them something to write about." I must admit that I used to think that about my first graders, so in those days I gave them "story starters." Donald Graves (1983) once referred to this as "writing welfare." We get kids dependent on assigned topics, and they come to believe that they don't have any ideas of their own.

S H O P T A L K

Graves, Donald H. *Experiment with Fiction.* Portsmouth, New Hampshire: Heinemann, 1989. *Investigate Nonfiction*, 1989.

Fifth-grade teacher Mary Kitagawa says of these books: "If you find you cannot get to a Donald Graves workshop as often as you'd like, the solution is to obtain some of his books and take them home. I especially like these two of the five-volume series, The Reading/Writing Teacher's Companion. Many chapters include *Actions*, which are suggestions and examples of activities. These make the text resemble a series of workshops with the author. The *Actions* are the type of hands-on experiences you'd do in 'A Day with Donald Graves' or classroom experiments you'd try between weekly support group meetings. Many are invitations to develop your own writing."

Student Writing Survey/Interest Inventory

Name _____ Date _____ Grade ____

1. Do you like to write? Why or why not?

2. Why do people write?

3. What makes a piece of writing effective?

4. What do you do especially well?

5. What are your favorite books?

6. What are you most curious about (what would you like to learn about)?

From *The Whole Language Catalog: Forms for Authentic Assessment* © 1994 edited by Lois Bridges Bird, Kenneth S. Goodman, and Yetta M. Goodman

Natalie Goldberg, author of two highly original writing guides, *Writing Down the Bones: Freeing the Writer Within* (1986) and *Wild Mind: Living the Writer's Life* (1990), says that the first order of business of writing is to "trust your own mind and have confidence in your own ideas."

Maureen White, K-8 Writing Coordinator for Haverhill Public Schools in Massachusetts, helps her students identify potential writing topics by asking them to reflect on their own writing process. She created the "Student Writing Survey/Interest Inventory" (1994) to help students reflect on writing, think about the links to reading, and identify topics they might want to explore in writing or through research. With this information in her files, she can help students get a jump start on writing when they become mired in their own indecision about what to write about. White also finds it helpful to ask students to complete the inventory at least twice a year and then compare the results. How have their interests changed? What do they know about the writing process later in the school year that they didn't know at the beginning? Older students can complete the form on their own. You can interview younger students, or ask parents or older students to assist if you can't find the time yourself.

Oakland, California, teacher Pam Bovyer Cook recommends the parent-teacher interview in the *Primary Language Record* (Barrs 1989). As described in the *Record*, Bovyer Cook finds interviewing parents about their children at the beginning of the school year a most effective way to find out about the child's home literacy experiences and interests. She suggests it's a real "paradigm shift" because the teacher listens while parents share all sorts of valuable information about their child, giving the teacher a "fuller picture" of the child.

If you still think kids need story starters, listen to what Donald Graves (1978) found in his extensive study of developing writers. "The data show that writers who learn to choose topics well make the most significant growth in both information and skills at the point of best topic." And there's more. "With best topic (meaning a topic that kids really care about), the child exercises strongest control, establishes ownership, and with ownership, pride in the piece." That's a convincing and reassuring research finding.

Sukar knows the importance of controlling topic choice. He transferred mid-year to Fair Oaks School in Redwood City, California. At his other school, students did not choose their own writing topics and for weeks, Sukar resisted. "My other teachers always told me what to write," he insisted. By April, he'd grown into controlling his own writing. He wrote this note to let his teacher know just how much he appreciated his newfound freedom.

Thank you for leting me grow my own stary I had fun riting my stary becuase it made me happy. The end.

I enjoyed reading your story Sukar. You can write one any time you'd like!

Find a Topic

What I'm going to do now is model for you how I launch a writer's workshop and help children identify the writing topics that they care about. The only difference is that I can't call you up to the front of the classroom and invite you to sit cross-legged with me in a cozy circle on the rug so that we can all see and hear each other. Otherwise, everything I'm going to describe now is exactly the way I do it with my students.

SHOPTALK

Learning Media. *Dancing with the Pen: The Learner as a Writer.* Wellington, New Zealand. Ministry of Education, 1993.

And dance is what you'll want to do after opening the covers of this beautifully written book. The text is graced with striking photographs of students as writers in action together with inspiring samples of children's writing. The lucid text helps teachers understand the writing process and how children learn to write. It also explains how to create a classroom environment that fosters writing, and provides practical strategies for supporting young writers. With this book as a partner, you and your students will learn to dance to your own writing rhythms.

I look carefully around the circle, making eye contact with each student, and then I begin to explain what it means to discover our writing selves. "Being a writer involves making lots of decisions," I say. "How are you going to begin your piece? How long will it be? Where will it take place? Who will read it? These are things I can't decide for you. Probably the first major decision you'll have to make is 'What am I going to write about?' I'm going to write, too, so let me share some of my ideas. These are things that I've been thinking about. They are ideas that I'd like to explore further in writing."

Lois's Topic List

1. **My Rotten Cold.** "I might write about being sick. I have a nasty cold just now and I'm so mad at myself. I pride myself on never getting sick, but thinking my stuffy nose was no more than bothersome hay fever, I paid it little attention and didn't fight back with my favorite cold-buster, mega-doses of vitamin C. Suddenly, my stuffy nose was joined by a fever and aches and chills, and I knew I'd been snagged by a cold. I haven't had a cold in so long, I've forgotten how dreadful they are. I could easily describe in self-pitying, red-nosed, sniveling detail how miserable I feel!

2. **Remodeling My House.** We're just in the initial stages of remodeling our home, and my husband and I are feeling overwhelmed with the details we need to consider. Suddenly I'm having anxiety attacks in the middle of the night because we haven't decided on what kind of molding should go around the doors. Yikes! We haven't even decided what kind of doors to use—hollow core or paneled? Who cares?! But for the next six months, it seems we're duty-bound to care about the selection and placement of nearly every nail.

3. **My Dog, the Thief.** My black Lab, Abby, is a thief. She spends her days on the prowl for food. Despite her girth, she's been known to jump from floor to chair to dinner table to grab a tasty tidbit left unattended for a moment. My parents visited us recently, and, one morning, I prepared a rather elaborate breakfast for my dad complete with a Spanish omelet, buttered English muffins, and coffee. Unaware of the need to vigilantly guard his food from Abby, he innocently rose from the table to get some cream for his coffee, leaving his breakfast unattended. Anticipating his delicious meal, he returned to find an empty plate, licked nearly spotless. All that remained was a residue of butter with one addition—a wiry black hair."

I want you—and my students—to understand that writers write best on topics they own.

These are topics I might write about. And you'll notice, they are all things that have really happened to me, things that I care about. That way it will be easy for me to write and to care about my writing.

In general, I give students about ten minutes to generate a list of topics. Most go right to work, jotting down five, six, even ten ideas. For those who sit before an empty page, I ask a few questions to get them started, "What do you like to do in your free time?" or "What do you know a lot about?" or "What's a good book you've read recently? What made it so good for you?"

I want you—and my students—to understand that writers write best on topics they own. This doesn't mean that you, or they, select topics in a void or without help. As you think about your own writing and help your students enter writing, you might keep these guidelines in mind.

- Value your own knowledge and firsthand experiences. Natalie Goldberg (1986) exhorts us to "trust our own minds and have faith in our own experiences." As Goldberg explains, we're "compost piles" of experiences—heaps of relationships, fractured dreams, missed appointments, midnight feedings, and so forth. Somewhere from deep within the warmth of our own lives, there's a story waiting to bloom.

Rachel Bullard, a second grader in Maureen Powell's class at Curtis Estabrook School in Brooklyn, New York, gives it to us straight. "When you're writing a story, don't just write anything down. Write about something you know. Write about your dog or your cat or your family or someone in your family. That's how you make stories more interesting."

```
┌─────────────────────────────────────────────────┐
│              D I A L O G U E                      │
│                                                   │
│  What might I write about? Take some time to jot  │
│  down a few topics. What's on my mind?            │
│                                                   │
│  _____ │
│                                                   │
│  _____ │
│                                                   │
│  At the top of your paper, write "Topic List" and │
│  keep a running list of topics as they come to    │
│  mind.                                            │
│                                                   │
│  _____ │
│                                                   │
│  _____ │
└─────────────────────────────────────────────────┘
```

• Explore your surroundings—inside and outside the classroom. As William Burroughs (1986) once said, "For Godsake, keep your eyes open. Notice what's going on around you." Where are you? What do you see? hear? feel? smell? sense? imagine? Toby Curry, who teaches sixth grade, suggests that a "simple bus or walking trip can be the perfect prompt for some delightful writing. Terrill Young had just graduated from middle school when he penned this touching poem about his city."

Detroit
by Terrill Young

Deep down in the heart of my city,
reflections of a gigantic mirror,
shows the elegant structures of downtown.
Abstract rivers flow as peaceful as can be.
The noise of the lunch hour traffic
Roars down the street.
Flashing lights of an EMS
Pass you heroically.
At night the city's vivid lights
Are like cat eyes shining.
On dark corners people socialize
In swarms like bees.
Stars make a glare that pierces air.
Will you dare to look into the reflections,
I know you'll care,
What's deep down in the heart of my city.

- Talk with others about your ideas. "Writing floats on a sea of talk," the great British educator James Britton (1970) reminds us. Talk with your colleagues, talk with your students. What are they writing about? What do they think of your ideas? Talk to write.

Nicole, a third grader in Barbara Nelson's class at Keeling Elementary in Tucson, Arizona, understands the influence of talking about writing on her development as an author. In this dedication to her published book, she acknowledges the many friends who helped her see her book through to a successful completion.

> I want to thank Token and his freinds for their wonderful ideas. I want to thank my DaD for the storis he told me when I was 5, 6, 7, and 8. I want to thank my teacher Mrs. Barbra Nelson for ecoraging me on thregh the dificcltys of this book. I also want to thank CS lewis for his wonderfol ideas. I want to thank Carissa Scott and Lisa Coda for sitting by me very pashontly giving me ideas for the ilistrashons. I want to thank My Grandpa and my DaD for sitting at my bed one night explaining to me the rools of publishing a book. I want to thank my hole theird grade class for complimenting me on my work. I am sorry if I missed enyone elts if I diD forget you pleas congrajalot yourselfc.
>
> froM Nicole

- Find answers to questions that interest you, read reference books; interview experts, listen to the news. The boundaries of our writing worlds can stretch as far as our minds can travel.

Once we've all generated a topic list, I invite my students to share. What ideas did they come up with? They can share with a partner. Sometimes we share as a whole class. Christophe talks about his trip to Great America. That reminds Jeremy of his mishap on a roller coaster. He adds that idea to his topic list. The talk and sharing help confirm our ideas—and stimulate new ones for us all.

After about ten minutes of general sharing, I quiet the children down and explain that we're going to choose one topic to write about. I return to my own writing and muse for a while as I demonstrate for them the business of topic selection. Which topic calls to me?

Since I'm thoroughly wrapped up in my cold just now—living in its stranglehold on my body—I think I'll write about it. I'll probably do a humorous piece with just the right veneer of self-pity to make me feel better.

Back in my classroom, I stretch out over my paper, and begin to write. It never fails—the writing energy I generate around my paper draws the students into their own writing. Soon, thirty other writers have followed my lead. Our classroom is electrified with writing power.

If it's the first time we've ever written together, I might limit this initial writing experience to about ten minutes. With more experienced writers, you can stretch it out to fifteen or twenty minutes or as long as your class seems engaged in their writing.

After our writing time, I pull the children back to the rug for our ritual closing. I end every writer's workshop with an "all-group share." The first time we share, we keep things simple. I explain that every time we write, we'll have the opportunity to share our writing with each other—as partners, in small groups, or with our whole class. No matter what else we do, however, we'll end every workshop together on the rug, sharing. Not everyone can share every day, but we'll take turns so that everyone who wants to share with the whole class will eventually have a chance.

The ground rules I set today for our all-group share carry us through the year. Sharing writing takes courage. Therefore, we accept each other's writing as gifts. We receive the gifts with love and care and compassion. We celebrate each other as writers. And later, as we become comfortable with our own writing and learn more about what makes writing effective, we can begin to make suggestions to individual writers that will help us all.

A Note about Writer's Notebooks

Several years ago, Lucy Calkins, the Director of the Teachers College Writing Project in New York City, and her colleagues began using writer's notebooks with their students, thus narrowing the gap even more between what kids do in school and what professional writers do on the job. What is a writer's

SHOPTALK

Wilde, Jack. *A Door Opens: Writing in Fifth Grade.* Portsmouth, New Hampshire: Heinemann, 1993.

Jack Wilde is a fifth-grade teacher at the Bernice A. Ray School in Hanover, New Hampshire. He presents classroom writing practices—poetry, report writing, persuasive writing, and writing across the curriculum—in the context of his own classroom, making this book especially practical for teachers. Although Wilde works with fifth graders, his book serves as an instructional map for elementary and middle school teachers.

It's important to work as a writer alongside your students.

notebook? It's a tool many professional writers use to capture their thoughts, feelings, and ideas in writing. The notebook is a place to think on paper, to ask questions, explore ideas, play with language, muse, hope, and dream. Joanne Hindley (1996) offers this helpful definition: "A writer's notebook can be many things: a place to make mistakes, to experiment, to record overheard conversations or family stories, to remember an inspiring quotation, to free associate, to ask questions, to record beautiful or unusual language, to jot down the seeds of unborn stories or story beginnings, to tell the truth or to lie, to record memories, to embellish memories…to think on the page so (your) notions of what's possible become less limited."

Instead of creating topic lists and collecting separate writing pieces in folders, many teachers are now opting to use writer's notebooks. Do what works best for you and your students. Read about writer's notebooks to learn more about the possible advantages they offer over writing folders. Then make your own adaptations to fit your writer's workshop.

It's important to work as a writer alongside your students. You don't have to write to publish (although it's fabulous to consider setting a publishing goal for yourself). But do write and do share your writing with others including your students. From inside your own writing self, you'll know so much better how to help your students find their writing selves.

Chapter 3

How To Design and Run a Writer's Workshop

by Greg Chapnick

Greg Chapnick is a good friend of mine. He is also a talented teacher, one who thoroughly enjoys helping his students become writers. I asked Greg to share with us how he runs a writer's workshop in his multigrade classroom at Charquin School in Hayward, California. As he assures you, he found his own way into writer's workshop. You'll want to consider creating your own writer's workshop with your students.

Let's start with a daily schedule. That is, how to structure the writer's workshop. There are no hard and fast rules here. This plan works for me, but you should make it fit your own and your students' needs. For example, in the beginning of the year I usually shorten most of the time periods, extending them as the students become more comfortable with the process. Sometimes I cut the mini-lesson or the "status-of-the-class" check (Atwell 1987). (Please refer to my Writer's Workshop Schedule on page 40.) It depends on what else is going on and how the class and I feel that day. I have my plan and I try to stick to it, but I know that being flexible will help all of us keep our sanity. You, too, will learn to adjust your schedule according to your students' needs.

Writer's Workshop Schedule

15 minutes: Silent Writing

Just as it says, no talking, no questions, no assistance, no nothing except quiet individual communing with your book or story.

10 minutes: Mini-lesson

Short direct instruction lesson on procedures, how-tos, grammar, punctuation, and spelling.

5 minutes: "Status-of-the-Class" Check

Quick, daily review of each student's plans for the period.

20 minutes: Writing, Conferencing, Editing, Publishing

Writing—pen or pencil making marks on paper.

Conferencing—quiet meeting with one or more partners to read and discuss a story written by a student.

Editing—proofreading for syntax, spelling, grammar, and punctuation.

Publishing the final draft—making a book of your story.

10 minutes: Whole-Class Group Conference

Entire class meets to hear and discuss a story.

Introducing the Workshop: Topic Selection

I always begin by sharing with my class how I prepared to introduce writer's workshop to them. I explain how I thought about three or four writing topics that I would want to write about and how I settled on one. If I'm feeling very confident, I'll even ask them to advise me on which topic sounds the most interesting. This is a set-up because I purposefully choose topics so that there's only one that cries out for being put to paper immediately. (A wise colleague calls this "stacking the deck" for children's learning.)

First, I tell them about a serious and potentially gripping story, like one of my son's operations. I speak softly, telling them how scary it was and how I worried about my son. By this time I have their full attention. I quietly tell them that this is a very important story to me, but that I am not quite ready to write about it, yet. Perhaps I will be later in the year.

Then, I talk about a potentially exciting idea that I've seen or heard about on television, like rock climbing or race car driving. I explain that it really looked exciting, and just watching it, I could almost imagine myself doing it. Unfortunately, I tell them, I don't have any personal experience with it so I'm not sure that I could write effectively about such a topic.

Finally, I tell them a funny story—some terrible mistake I've made trying to fix an appliance or something crazy my dogs have done. This year, I can write about the return of Mr. Fix-It. Our hero deletes all the files from the aforementioned wise colleague's computer while "customizing" her desktop. I make sure I am particularly animated when I tell this story so that my audience is subtly, or not so subtly, persuaded to ask me to choose this topic to write about. It doesn't take much to influence a group of children to choose the funny story over the others, so I don't lay it on too thick.

After choosing my topic, I invite my students to experience the same process, telling their stories to a partner or to the whole class. How much talking goes on before writing, and in what configuration, varies from year to year. For instance, this year I have a third- through sixth-grade class in an alternative program full of extremely bright and verbal children who have done very little formal writing. The contrast with my previous classes is so noticeable that I knew this class had to start with talking rather than writing. So, instead of introducing my story and then asking the kids to quickly think of their own stories and begin writing, I spent a lot of time talking about my story. I then invited them to talk to each other about their stories. We did this for at least a week before we ever put a pen to paper.

It was really important for these kids to talk first. Talking and sharing serves the double purpose of allowing children to see that they, too, have stories to write. It also helps us build our classroom community. As a child talks about a particular event in his or her life, you can see the others nodding their heads in agreement as they recognize a similar event in their lives. (Often this can result in a "writing virus" with whole segments of the class writing similar stories.)

S H O P T A L K

Graves, Donald. *Writing: Teachers and Children at Work*. Portsmouth, New Hampshire: Heinemann, 1983.

This may be the book that started it all, that revolutionized everything we know about writing and the teaching of writing. Graves explains the writing process and how to make it work in the classroom. He recommends that teachers write. It's much easier to work with students as writers if you understand your own writing. Graves also insists that there is practically no limit to what kids can do as writers. "At every single point in our research," he writes, "we've underestimated what kids can do."

I usually suggest making a semantic map or web of their stories. This is a simple chart with the title in the middle and bubbles or circles coming off it with key words or phrases. The idea is to have some kind of plan before you start writing. Lists work, too. I've found that many kids don't like this part, so I don't belabor the point. It's a quick sketch, not a first draft. They do like sharing their semantic maps with the whole class, and it's a great way to build confidence as they speak to everyone. However, requiring them to make a map can also be counterproductive, especially on the first few stories, so you have to be flexible and take your cues from your own students.

After we talk a lot, choose topics, and web our stories, we finally begin writing. Whether it's right away or days later, at some point I ask the students to begin writing. Some teachers stop their students soon after they've started writing and ask them to read the beginnings of their compositions to a partner and then try to write a new lead. It's a way to help kids discover the different options for beginning a story, but I haven't had much success with this early in the school year. Other teachers just let their students write until they drop. It's up to you. Experiment. Have fun! It's not brain surgery—at least in the conventional sense.

I try to structure my curriculum so kids can finish projects, but not processes.

Write, Write, Write

Let's assume that somehow you've gotten through the introduction to writer's workshop, and it's the second day. Inevitably, one or two or huge masses of students will tell you they have finished their story. "I'm done. What do I do now?" This brings us to a basic law in my universe: "You are never finished in this class."

I try to structure my curriculum so kids can finish projects, but not processes. "Finished your story? Great! Choose another topic and start another writing project." At some point, this response becomes so tiresome for students that they stop asking and just do it.

For the first two weeks, sometimes more, I just tell my students to keep writing one written composition after another. I do this for two reasons. First, I want them to have a number of compositions from which to choose before getting to the conference and editing stages. Second, I want to build up the anticipation to a fever pitch before I let them get on to the other stages of the writing process. Second drafts and proofreading are not their favorite steps, so I try to make it seem as exciting as possible. It's a fine line. You don't want to postpone it too long or they'll get bored and stop writing. There has to be a payoff before they peak.

Another law: "Fiction is hard. Write about yourself first." Most kids, given a chance, will write a fantasy story or a monster story or a super-hero-monster-fantasy story. One school of thought says let them write whatever they want because they'll be motivated. The other school says hold off on the fiction for a while because even the best fiction draws from the author's own experience, and it's best to work on that first. I come from the latter school. Unless you have an unusually accomplished young writer, the fiction you'll get will be completely illogical, epic-length tales of death, destruction, and pre-adolescent fantasy.

Law number three: "First drafts are messy." And a corollary: "Erasers are illegal on first drafts." This one can get you into trouble if the kids take the "messy" part literally, which many of them are naturally inclined to do. The idea is to free up the writer, unleash the soul of the artist, and all that creative stuff. I make a big joke out of threatening to break off the erasers from everyone's pencils, but the real point of this is to discourage the kids from trying to be perfect the first time and allowing you, as the teacher and chief editor, to trace their thought processes through all their existing writing as much as possible. When they erase things, it is impossible to tell what changes have been made. I suggest a neat line through parts that are changed, but I'll take a sloppy, scratchy squiggle over erasing. It's not that I examine in detail every change every writer makes, but sometimes I learn things about a writer's thinking that I would never discover if the change was erased.

Field Notes: Teacher-To-Teacher

How do kids feel about writer's workshop? I asked my students and they were uniformly enthusiastic about our writer's workshop. Here are some of their comments:

"You can't show your own ability by using a textbook, but when you write, you find out what you're capable of, and you find out about your own mistakes."

"You learn without realizing you're learning in the writer's workshop. A textbook is boring."

"I'm still getting my language skills, but in a fun way."

"It enables us to be more creative and express ourselves more freely. We learn by doing (writing!) instead of working out of a textbook."

Ruth Taravella
District #70
Pueblo, Colorado

Mini-Lessons

"Don't force mini-lessons." This law is for me. I say it over and over again to myself, year after year.

Mini-lessons should be what they sound like, short lessons. Whenever possible and appropriate, I try to demonstrate an instructional point using student writing or my own. Having students conduct the lesson, showing some skill they've mastered or some idea they've discovered can be particularly effective. Of course, I only use student writing for positive reasons—to demonstrate a writing breakthrough or triumph—never to showcase mistakes a student has made.

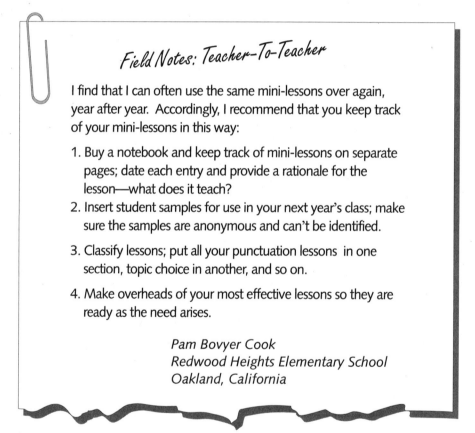

Field Notes: Teacher-To-Teacher

I find that I can often use the same mini-lessons over again, year after year. Accordingly, I recommend that you keep track of your mini-lessons in this way:

1. Buy a notebook and keep track of mini-lessons on separate pages; date each entry and provide a rationale for the lesson—what does it teach?
2. Insert student samples for use in your next year's class; make sure the samples are anonymous and can't be identified.
3. Classify lessons; put all your punctuation lessons in one section, topic choice in another, and so on.
4. Make overheads of your most effective lessons so they are ready as the need arises.

Pam Bovyer Cook
Redwood Heights Elementary School
Oakland, California

Status of the Class

This can take anywhere from three to thirty-three minutes. It's supposed to be a quick check-in where students tell you what they will be doing during the writer's workshop period. We do a quick run around the room, and every student explains his or her plans for writer's workshop that day. I quickly jot down their plans on my chart, which I keep handy on a clipboard. When check-in takes three minutes, it's great. It focuses the students, it focuses you, and it provides a record so you can keep track of students who have trouble finishing stories. When you notice that a student has changed topics every day

Writing Workshop: Status of the Class

Legend: 1. New text   3. Conferencing   5. Revising
               2. Working on draft   4. Using Technology   6. Editing

Names	Date									
1										
2										
3										
4										
5										
6										
7										
8										
9										
10										
11										
12										
13										
14										
15										
16										
17										
18										
19										
20										
21										
22										
23										
24										
25										
26										
27										
28										
29										
30										
31										
32										
33										
34										
35										

SHOPTALK

Atwell, Nancie. *In the Middle: Writing, Reading, and Learning with Adolescents.* Portsmouth, New Hampshire: Heinemann, 1987.

Middle school teacher Ruth Ann Blynt loves Nancie's book. She explains:

"I spent late summer and early fall with my Nancie Atwell 'bible' tucked under my arm, hoping to absorb her philosophy. I followed her advice to the letter, checking and rechecking with it after each new writing/reading workshop class. I haven't spent so much time with a book since I read Dr. Spock and Karen Pryor while breast-feeding my firstborn."

I know kindergarten teachers who are just as enthusiastic as Blynt when it comes to this book. Nancie's writing workshop philosophy, structure, and strategies work for students of all ages.

for three weeks or has been on the same story for three months, it's time for a not-so-gentle reminder. The "Status of the Class" chart is one way to help you notice these situations—and they *will* occur.

I fill in what they say ("My Trip to Great America, Draft 1" or "The Time I Fell Off My Bike, Conference") next to their names with the days of the week on top. Once the kids get the pattern, it goes quickly, especially on successive days when you can just draw an arrow or change to the next stage of the process instead of writing the entire title over and over. The basic question is "What are you going to do today?"

"I don't know," or "Huh?" are not acceptable answers.

In the beginning of this process, I have showed the class a poster I've made that, lists the stages or steps involved in writer's workshop.

- Find a topic, make a map
- Write (1st draft)
- Conference
- Revise (2nd, 3rd...drafts)
- Edit, Proofread
- Publish

Having the list in front of them helps the students in the beginning, but after a while, it's really for visiting parents because the kids know what they have to do. In order to publish a story, an author must go through each one of the stages. No story makes it past the editor-in-chief (me) without going through each step at least once, and sometimes more than once.

Conferencing

Okay, so you're two weeks into the school year, and "Write a new story" won't cut it any longer. It's time to bite the bullet and introduce conferencing. Right now I'm talking about content conferences rather than editing/proof-reading/spelling/grammar conferences or evaluation conferences. This is "What do you think of my story?" time.

Conferences can be with partners, with small groups, or with the whole class. Regardless of the grouping, the format is the same:

1. The author reads the story aloud.
2. The audience tells what they heard.
3. The audience makes comments or suggestions.
4. The author tells what she or he will do next—which comments she or he will respond to, and what changes will be made.

The point of a content conference is constructive criticism.

I use the form on page 49 for conferencing. The author fills all this in because it's hard to decipher another person's handwriting and unconventional spelling. This also ensures that the writer really pays attention to what the partners say.

The point of a content conference is constructive criticism. This is not a familiar concept for most students. Conferencing can easily degenerate into an attack on the author that rarely, if ever, has anything to do with the story that has been written. You want to encourage student authors to read their stories, and they won't do that unless they are reasonably sure that the response will be gentle and supportive. It's another one of those fine lines. You don't want to set anyone up for an attack, but you also want the audience to be helpful. When someone tells an author that everything she writes is wonderful and perfect, that's not much better than tearing everything to shreds. It may be good for popularity in the classroom but not for developing writing skills.

A couple of years ago, I made a change that completely transformed my conferences from unproductive popularity contests into one of my most effective teaching tools. Up until then, the first question on my conference form was, "What did you like about the story?" Then I changed it to "What did you hear about the story?" Worded this way, the question focuses the author and the audience on the words in the story—what happened, how it happened, whom it happened to, and so on—rather than whether the characters and actions are cool or gross. You want conference partners to tell the author what they heard, so the author can tell if that is the same story that he or she intended to write. "Is that what you really wanted to say? Because we heard this other thing."

This is all we do the first few times. No reactions or judgments at all. Later, after the students get comfortable with the process, with me, and with each other, I introduce comments and suggestions and show them ways we might guide the writer. For some kids, being told how to change their writing can be a very delicate issue, so I err on the side of going slowly. Hence, my next law: "You *could* change this, not you *should* change this."

Encourage possible improvements but don't dictate them. I want student authors to begin thinking about and evaluating their own work. If you strongly suggest a change, there is a risk that the author will make the change just to please you. Other times, a student's suggestion to an author may be on target, but the author won't even consider it because the suggestion hurt his or her feelings.

One final point: children generally love hearing and responding to their classmates' writing, but aren't as fond of listening to the teacher point out things. In whole-class conferences, I try to have the author run the show while I record comments on the conference form. The student reads the story, everyone else listens, we applaud, and then respond with our comments and suggestions. I speak up to move things along or to elaborate on particular comments. I also highlight concepts or skills as they come up in the sharing, and point out that the particular idea we are talking about is applicable to everyone's writing.

Conferencing Form

Author _____ Date _____

Title _____ Partner(s)_____

What did your partner hear and learn from your story?

_____

_____

_____

_____

_____

What questions or suggestions does your partner have about your story?

_____

_____

_____

_____

_____

What do you (the author) plan to do next?

_____

_____

_____

_____

_____

Revision

As with conferencing, the unfamiliar part of revision for students is really the idea itself. A lot of "unteaching" can be involved to convince kids that revision does not mean that there is something wrong with their first draft. Far too often, I find that students expect their work to be "right" the first time. I expect the students to revise not only in writer's workshop, but in all the writing they do across the curriculum. I try to develop the idea that second, third, and even further drafting is not merely making corrections, but is a natural and desirable part of the writing process.

Stories can go through more than one conference and more than two drafts, but nothing gets published with a single draft. Second drafts for elementary students are not usually true second drafts as adult writers think of them. Occasionally you have a student who gets it and makes substantive changes

I have no doubt that students who participate in a writer's workshop for several years begin to understand more fully the revision process.

between drafts, but most often the revisions are simple additions or dele-tions. I have no doubt that students who participate in a writer's workshop for several years begin to understand more fully the revision process. Most of the kids I have are essentially first-time writers. The ones who aren't are obvious. You can see it in their first piece. And when a student author's piece has "voice," it jumps right off the page at you. Even these writers, though, may be unfamiliar with revision.

I introduce revision by demonstrating the process with my own writing. I read my first draft to the class, absorb their comments, and go home to write the second draft based on their comments. A few days later, I read my sec-ond draft to the kids, showing them on an overhead projector how I incor-porated their suggestions and altered my text. Students can see that it takes time and work to revise a piece. There is some "set-up" because I purposely write the first draft in a dull and predictable manner that will cry out for needed revision.

Editing

Let's cut to the chase—this part is not a lot of fun because it can be a lot of tedious work for everyone. I don't know any way around it, though. At some point, unless you just want to let any old piece of writing get published and dis-played, you and your students have to do some work examining and cor-recting grammar, punctuation, and spelling. My best advice is to keep it as simple as possible.

I use the "Editing Checklist" to help the students proofread and edit their own writing.

Upper elementary students don't get much farther than the items on the checklist. In addition, I teach basic grammar, focusing on verb tense, verb agreement, and proper use of adjectives and adverbs. Older or more ac-complished students can go farther. Younger students may not go this far. Really young ones, kindergarten or first grade, may revise or edit less. First-grade teacher Sherry Swain reminds us that it is "during the editing phase

---

Editing Checklist

Author _____ Date _____

Title of Story _____

☐ I have reread my story to make sure there are no missing words.

☐ I have checked my story for run-on and incomplete sentences.

☐ I have indented each paragraph.

☐ I have used capital letters for names, places, titles, and the beginning of
    sentences.

☐ I have checked all punctuation: periods, commas, quotation marks,
    question marks, and exclamation points are in the right places.

☐ I have circled all the words I think are misspelled.
    The correct spellings are below: (Put more words on back of checklist.)

_____ _____ _____

_____ _____ _____

_____ _____ _____

---

that children learn to heed conventions in their writing—and increase their comprehension." On any individual story, I also limit the number of types of corrections, besides spelling, to one or two. Any more than that overwhelms most student writers.

I tend to value editing your own story over peer editing, but both can be worthwhile. There's no "right" way to do it. Students can edit their own work or another student's work, alone or in small groups, once a day or once a week, or only when publishing. Some teachers have rotating "editors-of-the-week" and editing tables. It seems more difficult to spot your own errors than someone else's, but I like the idea of examining your own mistakes. If I am trying to encourage children to value their mistakes as learning tools, constructing their own knowledge as they go along, it makes more sense to have them identify and correct their own errors.

When a story has been revised and edited, it can be put in the "To Be Published" basket for the editor-in-chief to evaluate. Most of the stories that are put in this basket are immediately returned to the student because very little or no proofreading has been done. This happens a lot. I have to be really ruthless or I will be inundated with hundreds of quickly written and quickly edited stories. I make sure that from the start, then, that I am vigilant about students doing enough work on their own before I even look at the story.

Field Notes: Teacher-To-Teacher

Before my second- or third-grade students can ask a classmate to help them edit, or have an editing conference with me, I insist that they independently proofread their pieces for missing words. They also underline words that they know are misspelled. Of course before they can do this, I have had several mini-lessons modeling how to proofread. An editing checklist is posted in the room which lists the skills that are expected of everyone. As children learn new skills, such as the use of quotation marks, they add those skills to a personal checklist in their writing folders.

Laura Schwartzberg
P.S. 234
New York, New York

This may seem difficult at first, but after seeing a few dozen stories with "the" and "is" missing from sentences and finding simple words, including the author's own name, misspelled, it gets easier to evaluate stories with a quick look. Eventually, though, a story will make its way into the basket that merits your full attention because it is ready to be published. I try to limit this to ten stories per student per year. If that doesn't sound like a lot, try multiplying thirty-five times ten and then think about it. I also return stories that are assembled improperly. I get tired of trying to figure out which draft is which or where the editing checklist is. I ask that stories be assembled in reverse order of their creation, so the first thing I see is an editing checklist on top of a second (or last) draft.

Spelling

This is it—the big issue. It's such a big issue that I've assigned it a separate section, even though it's really part of the editing process. Children can learn to spell by trying out their own versions of spelling a word (invented spelling), testing and confirming those spellings with a dictionary, and mostly by reading a lot and seeing conventional spelling. Good spellers can see, almost feel in their stomachs, a misspelling; something doesn't look or feel right about the word. That comes from lots of experience of having seen conventional spelling in published books and practicing writing on their own. Some people simply aren't good spellers and never will be. That's where dictionaries and spell-checkers come into play. We spend a lot of time working on spelling. The students write for at least an hour a day, and spelling is a very important part of that writing.

Spelling *is* important. I don't emphasize it on first drafts, but I do value it for effective communication. It's a difficult issue. If you have to give spelling tests, go ahead. It won't hurt the kids to memorize a few words each week, but it has little to do with becoming a good speller and even less to do with becoming a good writer.

My spelling law: "Don't spell it yourself!" (you being the teacher) and its corollary: "Spell it yourself!" (you being the student). This is a law that I enforce heavily, and only break when I'm totally exhausted. Walking around the class, I almost never spell a word for students. I encourage using the dictionary and tell students to use their own heads and stomachs (that feeling that a word doesn't look right) over a friend or just guessing. I do encourage students to teach grammar and punctuation to each other, but I try to instill self-sufficiency (and encourage the use of a dictionary) for spelling.

My favorite response to a "How do you spell it?" question is to ask, "How do you think it's spelled?" or "What do you think the first/second/next letter is?" Most of the time the kids have a good idea of the correct spelling or something close. If they are close, I tell them to write it three times on scratch paper, see which one looks best, and confirm it with a dictionary. This is remarkably effective, but it does take time, and the time spent doing it rather than the job per se is what most of your students will fight. If they can learn strategies for quick use of a dictionary, they will be more apt to use one. Spell-checkers are another matter. It's like calculators—you can't fight progress. But at least students have to make a stab at spelling the word before they can use the spell-checker.

Spelling is *important.*

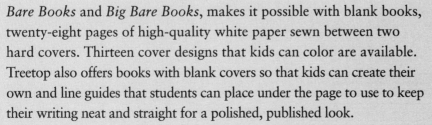

SHOPTALK

Treetop Publishers. *Bare Books* and *Big Bare Books*. Racine, Wisconsin: Treetop Publishing.

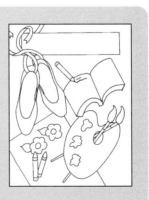

What better way to celebrate your students' authorship than to give them a bound, hardcover book in which to publish their written creations? Treetop Publishing, the creator of *Bare Books* and *Big Bare Books*, makes it possible with blank books, twenty-eight pages of high-quality white paper sewn between two hard covers. Thirteen cover designs that kids can color are available. Treetop also offers books with blank covers so that kids can create their own and line guides that students can place under the page to use to keep their writing neat and straight for a polished, published look.

When I'm editing a story as editor-in-chief, I always choose the least intrusive method of helping with spelling. First I'll count the misspelled words and write the number in a circle at the top of the page. The next step would be to circle some of the words. The most intrusive method is to correct it myself. I only do that at certain points on certain stories for certain students, usually because one of us is exhausted, frustrated, or both.

I try to keep a separate color for my editing marks, so I pick one that my students are unlikely to use—green. There's always that one kid, though, who finds a green pen (mine, usually) and throws a monkey wrench into the system.

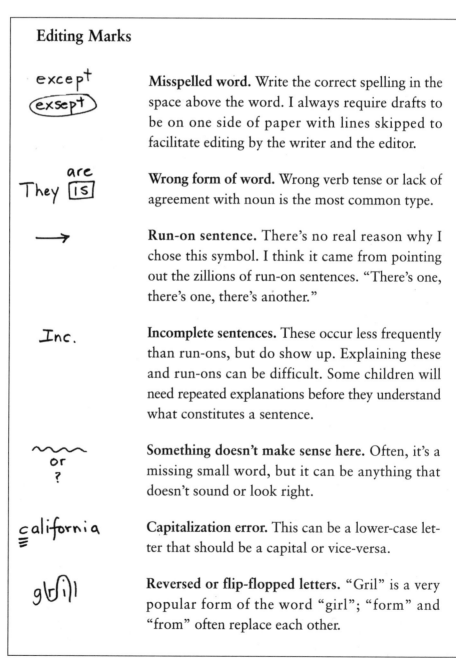

Editing Marks

Misspelled word. Write the correct spelling in the space above the word. I always require drafts to be on one side of paper with lines skipped to facilitate editing by the writer and the editor.

Wrong form of word. Wrong verb tense or lack of agreement with noun is the most common type.

Run-on sentence. There's no real reason why I chose this symbol. I think it came from pointing out the zillions of run-on sentences. "There's one, there's one, there's another."

Incomplete sentences. These occur less frequently than run-ons, but do show up. Explaining these and run-ons can be difficult. Some children will need repeated explanations before they understand what constitutes a sentence.

Something doesn't make sense here. Often, it's a missing small word, but it can be anything that doesn't sound or look right.

Capitalization error. This can be a lower-case letter that should be a capital or vice-versa.

Reversed or flip-flopped letters. "Gril" is a very popular form of the word "girl"; "form" and "from" often replace each other.

SHOPTALK

Brady, Sandra. *Let's Make Books*. Dubuque, Iowa: Kendall/Hunt Publishing, 1992.

Bookmaking affords a high level of student involvement, problem solving, and natural integration of reading, writing, skills, and content. *Let's Make Books* makes getting into this vital process easy. The book has thirty-eight pages of ways to bind children's own books; all twenty-five methods have large illustrations and step-by-step instructions. There are flow charts, checklists, and actual student examples to guide teacher and student through all phases of the bookmaking process, including forming and developing ideas, writing, revising, and final binding. The book is especially visual, as research suggests that graphics facilitate understanding. A cartoon character, Dr. Book Lady, guides the reader through monitoring, evaluation, quality control, and sharing. *Let's Make Books* shows how bookmaking can be a fun-filled, interactive learning process that both children and adults will love.

I keep a binder where I make notes about each student's work—how they've improved, where they need improvement, a few comments about the story and its style. From repeated error, I've learned that these notes need to be brief and written at the time you look at the story. Remembering long analyzes and an individual story even the next day are impossible tasks unless you have a photographic memory. It's up to you, though. If you find it fun, do it.

Publishing

I try to make publishing a book like creating a work of art. Mainly, I do this because my art program is so pitiful (but I'm working on it) that I take any opportunity to connect drawing and painting to my regular curriculum. At this point, all revising and editing should be complete.

Computers are wonderful for publishing. Kids love to type and print out their stories. Problems arise, however, if you don't have access to enough computers. Computer publishing can be time consuming and whoever gets there first tends to monopolize the machine. One teacher I know has one student dictate while the second types. This gets two students involved and can speed up the process.

I suggest that my students publish on half-size sheets of paper whether it's by hand or on the computer. I like the small size because it's similar to the paperback novels they read, it doesn't take up as much room on a bulletin board or shelf, and because it makes the book look more like a book and less like a report. I do let students publish in any format they choose, however. If you have access to a binding machine or laminating machine, you can do a nicer job than with just a stapler. There are also companies that will take your originals and bind them into hardback covers if you're so inclined.

My last two laws: "You may not spend the rest of your life publishing that book," and "Your attitude is the most important element of a successful writer's workshop."

Having a good attitude yourself about writer's workshop makes all the difference.

Having a good attitude yourself about writer's workshop makes all the difference. That means encouraging your kids to write, valuing their ideas and stories, and providing them with support without doing it for them. This is what it takes to have a successful writing program. If you have a bad attitude, it doesn't matter how clever and logical your systems and charts and folders are, the writing will still suffer. When I'm enthusiastic, so are the kids. When I think the whole thing is a drag and a bore, they pick up on that and follow my lead.

Provide time for your students to write, allow them to make mistakes, and, if possible, show them that you do all these things, too. There's nothing like firsthand experience to see what it's like for your students, especially if you haven't written much before. They'll love it when you show them all the mistakes you make and all the struggles you have with your own writing. Sharing your writing with your students is a very effective teaching tool.

The best advice I can offer is to relax and have a good time. I'm not always successful at that, but it's what I aim for. Your kids will pick up your comfort or your discomfort and amplify it. If you view writing as natural, enjoyable, relevant, and therapeutic, they will, too. Celebrate each other's creations. Work hard...and have fun.

SHOPTALK

Henderson, Kathy. *Market Guide for Young Writers*, 2d ed. Belvidere, New Jersey: Shoe Tree Press, 1988.

This useful book offers extensive advice for young writers on how to get their work published. In addition to an annotated list of over one hundred publications, the book includes helpful hints from students and professional editors, lists of contests and markets, ideas on manuscript preparation, and more.

Chapter 4

What Writers Need

In sixth grade, I was an avid fan of Nancy Drew. I spent my allowance to support a two-book-a-week habit. Not surprisingly, when my teacher, Mrs. Philipps, required us to write a story, I wrote my own Nancy Drew-like mystery thriller entitled "Tic Tac Toe, Three in a Row!" It opened in a Chinese restaurant with the heroine (a thin disguise of twelve-year-old me) finding a fortune tucked inside a fortune cookie. However, it wasn't a fortune at all! It was a hastily scrawled message begging for help. My twenty-page novella took off from there. Once I penned the dramatic conclusion, I turned in the results of my two-day writing fervor and eagerly awaited Mrs. Philipps' response. One week later, she handed the story back to me, smiling. Imagine my delight as I opened up its manila cover to discover this message, written in Mrs. Philipps' flowery cursive, "I can't wait to read your published novels some day."

Nearly thirty years later, I've never received a better response to my writing. Indeed, Mrs. Philipps' praise for that one story has carried me through every writing project I've tackled since (although I have yet to write a novel!). Mrs. Philipps helped me believe in myself as a writer.

Writers crave response. And a thoughtful, sensitive response nudges our students closer to an ability to control writing. If our students "ached with caring" as they were writing, then, as Mem Fox exhorts, "we must ache with caring as we respond to their writing."

This chapter will explain how to respond with caring to your students' writing. You'll learn how to balance your thoughtful, sensitive response with the supportive instruction they need to develop as more effective writers. What do writers need? We can pare down their needs to three essentials:

1. A real audience that listens intently.
2. A response to the specifics of their writing.
3. Help on deciding next steps with their writing.

Listen Hard To Respond Well

Listening to young authors is a challenge. First, as every teacher knows, there are days (perhaps most days) when finding five minutes of uninterrupted time to spend with one student is next to impossible. And, in your eagerness to complete the conference before moving on to the next student, you may seize control of the writing and fire off suggestions to the author before he or she has even finished reading it out loud. I know because I've done it. Your goal as a writing teacher is to let the child read, share, and explain. You, the teacher, listen. That's hard for some teachers to do! But listening is the first step in becoming an effective teacher of writing. As you initiate a writing conference with a student, try these three simple steps:

1. Listen to what the child has to say about his or her piece.
2. Tell the child what you understand.
3. Ask the child to clarify or expand on what you don't understand.

Carol Avery (1993), who works with her first grade writers in William Nitrauer School in Lancaster, Pennsylvania, explains that she doesn't come to each writing conference with a long list of questions to ask of the student author. Rather, over the years of working with young writers, she's developed a repertoire of writing questions that helps her nudge her first graders forward in specific directions. If she wants to

- identify the writer's purpose, she asks: "What's this writing about? What's the best part of this piece?"
- discover how things are going for the writer, she asks: "Where are you right now? What's the best thing you've written so far?"
- help the writer nail down a direction for the writing, she asks: "What will you do next? What are your plans for this piece?"

Avery maintains that her goal is not to teach the writing, but to teach the writer; to focus intently on what the writer is trying to say. The potential and stimulus for revision lie in the discrepancy (and the tension it creates for the writer) between what the writer actually wrote and what he or she intended to write. Jeremy reads his funny piece to you. It's a rambling account of how he dropped his baseball cap in the killer whale pool at Marine World. As you listen hard to his piece, you have trouble following the story line. It's not clear to you how the cap landed in the pool. Once Jeremy has finished reading, you explain to him what you understood about his story. He realizes that what he wrote doesn't quite match what he wanted to say. At that point of realization, he may decide that he needs to revise his piece to clarify his story. In a writing conference, we focus on our students like Jeremy, we listen hard to their writing, we respond with sensitivity and caring, and then, as Avery assures us, we can trust that their writing will evolve.

Every time you respond to a student's writing, you are demonstrating *how* to respond. With time and discussion, your students will internalize your response and learn to respond to each other's writing. Writers need a real audience. Don't limit your students' audience to you alone. Be sure to build time into every writer's workshop for an all-group share. Just as my students and I would begin our writer's workshop sitting in a cozy circle on the rug, we ended our workshop together on the rug. The children knew that during our all-group share, we had time for just four children to read aloud. That meant that children who wanted to share had to write their names in the four slots on the blackboard under "All-Group Share." It also meant that they had to practice reading their writing aloud to themselves several times so that when it was their turn to read out loud in front of the class, they were prepared. New York City teacher Laura Schwartzberg asks her second and third graders to read their work to at least one other person before they share it with the whole class.

Writers need a real audience.

Field Notes: Teacher-To-Teacher

How do you teach children to be specific as they respond to a peer author? Model specific responses for them! Show them again and again what it means to provide an author with a response that includes real information about the details of the writing. When they are responding to a peer author, my students begin with the statement "I heard…" and then tell the author just exactly what they heard as the author was reading his or her piece aloud. Eventually my students learn that "I liked your whole piece" is not an effective way to respond. Another point—if a listener was unable to follow the author's piece, he or she can say "I'm confused by…"

Laura Schwartzberg
P.S. 234
New York, New York

More experienced writers can also begin to identify what they want their audience to listen for. For example, Darius explains that he's writing a letter to the police chief asking him to send officers to patrol the school grounds at night. Drug dealers have been congregating on the grounds and leaving litter which the children encounter the next morning. He asks his audience to listen to his summary of the problem. Has he provided the police chief with enough background information? If not, what additional information should he add?

Children can also respond to each other's writing as partners. Some teachers invite children to chat about their writing any time the urge arises. Others prefer a more controlled environment. For example, you might explain to your students that peer conferences take place only in conferencing corners set up in the four corners of the classroom. As there are only four corners, this means that only four peer conferences can occur at a time. Additionally, you may monitor the time students can spend in peer conferences, setting a time limit of ten or fifteen minutes. To help establish guidelines, you may also find it helpful to give children a conferencing form. The form helps the writing partners focus on the business at hand and helps you see what transpired during the conference. Take a look at the three forms I've included.

Peer Conferencing

Name_____

Date	Topic	Partner's Initials	Suggestions

From *The Whole Language Catalog: Forms for Authentic Assessment* © 1994 Lois Bridges Bird, Kenneth S. Goodman, and Yetta M. Goodman.

Peer Conferencing Guidelines

Speak in quiet voices during conferencing. Other writers may be drafting, and it's hard to think when your thoughts are interrupted. Support each other by sharing your strategies.

Writer

1. **Share your work with another writer.** Read your own piece to the listener. You may want to ask the listener for help on a particular aspect of the piece, such as "Let me know if I've been less wordy this time."

2. **Listen carefully to the comments of the listener.** You may take notes on the suggestions to consider using them.

3. **Decide how or if to use the conferencing suggestions.** Remember, the purpose of conferencing is to lead the writer directly to revising (adding, deleting, changing) your text.

Listener

1. **Look at and listen to the writer who is sharing.** Listen carefully and take notes so that you can point out places in the piece where you thought the writing worked well. You may ask the writer to repeat a part, read more slowly, loudly, etc.

2. **Tell the writer what you heard.** Tell the writer a detail that you liked about the text. Be sure to use specifics, such as "I enjoyed the description of your school's locker room as 'pungent with the odor of old sweat socks.'"

3. **Say to the writer, "Tell me more about…" or "I'm confused by…"** Feel free to ask the writer any questions about his or her piece.

4. **Avoid telling the author what to do.** Avoid the words "you should." Remember, do not take away the writer's ownership.

From *The Whole Language Catalog: Forms for Authentic Assessment* © 1994 Lois Bridges Bird, Kenneth S. Goodman, and Yetta M. Goodman.

Greg Chapnick offers additional details on setting up successful all-group sharing sessions and peer conferences in Chapter 3.

Writers Crave Specifics

I said that writers crave a response to their writing. That's true. But what writers really crave is a response to the specifics of their writing. Let me explain. As a writer, which response would you find more helpful and satisfying?

1. "Wow! That was great!" or
2. "Wow! That was great! When you described the way you pushed your inner tube out over the edge of the slide and wrote about the great hand of gravity that reached up and jerked the inner tube down into a swirling cascade of water, I felt my stomach pitch forward just as though I had been on the inner tube with you."

It's obvious, of course. When we can identify for writers exactly what worked for us, then we help them improve as writers. They write more of what works for their audience and do less of what doesn't.

But what writers really crave is a response to the specifics of their writing.

We have to let go of old-fashioned notions that brilliant writers are born. Sure, some are, but it's equally true that brilliant writers can develop over time with lots of practice, opportunities to share their writing with a caring, responsive audience, and focused support from a competent writing teacher. It's difficult to share with a writer what really worked in his or her piece if you haven't a clue what constitutes effective writing. And, conversely, it's hard to make your writing work well for an audience if you don't know what qualities to strive for. So, one of our biggest jobs as writing teachers is to help our students understand the qualities of effective writing.

Help from the Pros
As often as possible, I turn to published authors for my writing lessons. I keep lists of authors' work I can use to teach specific lessons I want to share with my students. For a mini-lesson on leads, I turn to E. B. White. The character of Fern in *Charlotte's Web* startles readers as she shrieks at her Papa to spare the life of a runt pig. Katherine Paterson's descriptive opening passages carry us to Chesapeake Bay in *Jacob, Have I Loved*. And, as we turn to the first page in Scott O'Dell's *Island of the Blue Dolphins*, we find ourselves inside Karana's head as she surveys the rocky landscape of her island home. From White, Paterson, and O'Dell, my students discover different ways to invite readers into their written compositions.

Published authors are our best writing teachers for global writing concerns such as story leads, genre, and theme, as well as for such writing particulars as vocabulary, punctuation, spelling, and grammar; and don't forget literary devices such as simile, metaphor, and personification. Sixth-grade teacher Pam Bovyer Cook in Oakland, California, says that Roald Dahl and Scott O'Dell are "fabulous" for teaching simile. As you work with developing writers, you'll begin to identify patterns of writing issues that come up year after year. Match those patterns to published authors. E. B. White is a wonderful teacher for all aspects of writing, but I've used him especially for character development, dialogue, and description (read and enjoy his description of the Zuckerman's barn in *Charlotte's Web*; you see it, smell it, hear it, feel it—*experience* it!).

Help the Author

Your Name _____

Author's Name _____

Title of Paper Discussed _____

Directions: Choose a partner with whom to share your writing. As you complete each part of this worksheet, be sure to check it off in the Done column.

Done	Activity
	1. Author reads his or her paper out loud to you.
	2. You read author's paper out loud to him or her. As you read the paper, notice how the author develops his or her ideas.
	3. Find a sentence you especially like ("the golden line") and underline it. Explain to the author why you like this sentence.
	4. What compliment (+) can you give the author about this writing? What suggestions can you make to the author for making this writing even better (∗)? Summarize here: | +	∗ | |---|---| | | |
	5. If the author agrees, copy the golden line on a large piece of paper. (optional)

Now repeat the process with your own piece of writing.

SHOPTALK

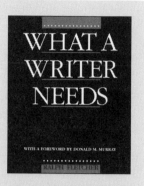

Fletcher, Ralph. *What a Writer Needs*. Portsmouth, New Hampshire: Heinemann, 1993.

Ralph Fletcher is one of my favorite writing teachers. One page into his *Walking Trees* (1991), I took the phone off the hook and read straight through to the last page. In *What a Writer Needs*, Fletcher offers a most helpful and complete appendix listing all sorts of references—fiction, nonfiction, picture books—which provide the lessons writers need. The appendix includes books that demonstrate powerful story beginnings and story endings; books that teach character development and voice; books that show-case setting; and books that celebrate unforgettable language. And, like *Walking Trees,* it's a stirring read.

Picture books are terrific teachers, too. As children reach the publishing phase and want to match their text with illustrations, it's very helpful to examine picture books and discuss the ways in which pictures support and enhance the story. New York City teacher Laura Schwartzberg recommends a "picture book study." After children have spent several weeks studying a wide variety of picture books, they are ready to create their own. Picture books also show us how to determine page breaks. That's a big decision. Where should one page end and another begin?

Don't forget the wide world of writing possibilities. Use published authors of all kinds to show your students "how it's done"—business letters, poems, persuasive essays, all about books, and so forth. Before young authors can effectively tackle different forms of writing, they need real-life examples and lots of talk about how and why the examples work. Oakland teacher Bovyer Cook uses a four-step process to help her students understand lessons from literature and begin to use them in their own writing.

1. I teach the concept or technique when we find it in a literature selection.
2. I invite my students to find other examples of it.
3. We make wall charts on which we copy the phrase or technique and identify the page and paragraph where we found it.
4. When the children begin to use the technique in their own writing—which they always do, of course—I'm delighted, and I let them know it.

Qualities of Effective Writing

Writing is so expansive and complicated and magical and precise and passionate and simple and…well, you get the idea. There's so much to know about writing and so much to learn about good writing. Although it seems hopelessly simplistic to capture all that good writing in one checklist, I'm going to try to do it because at least the list might be a jumping off point for you. "Qualities of Effective Writing" on page 66 draws from the work of writing experts such as Nancie Atwell, Lucy Calkins, Donald Graves, and Donald Murray. Note that the list not only includes the qualities and mechanics of an effective writing product, but also asks the evaluator to consider the process the author used in creating the composition.

For those of you eager to sharpen your understanding of writing, I offer this advice.

- Write, practice writing, share writing, and talk writing as often as possible.
- Read and reread your favorite authors. Keep a writing notebook in which you jot down favorite passages, choice of words, metaphors, and so forth. Go back and reread your notes. Work to understand why the authors touch you.
- Begin to build your own professional library of writing teachers. Strunk and White's *The Elements of Style* is a timeless favorite. William Zinsser's *On Writing Well: An Informal Guide To Writing Nonfiction* and Ralph Fletcher's *What a Writer Needs* are good books to begin with, too. Look also for Brenda Ueland's *If You Want To Write* and Anne LaMott's delightful *Bird by Bird: Some Instructions on Writing and Life*.
- Consider joining a writing group or participating in a local chapter of the National Writing Project. It's a terrific opportunity to become part of a community of writers. You'll write, share your writing, and listen and respond to others' writing. In the process, you'll grow in amazing ways in your understanding of and appreciation for writing.

Students Are Their Own Best Readers

What I know about writing I learned from my dad. As a well-known and respected historian who wrote for *The Saturday Review* and the *New York Times Book Review*, he has a musical ear and a sensitivity to and memory for beautiful language. He's also a kind and patient teacher. As a child, when I was grappling with a school writing assignment, I'd go to him for help. He sat in his rocking chair. I sat by his side. Together we read my school essays and reports, and he gently showed me what worked and what didn't. His comments helped me reshape my writing. More importantly, his comments taught me about the qualities of effective writing. From my dad, I learned

Qualities of Effective Writing

Name _____ Date _____ Grade _____

Quality of Expression

- ☐ inclusion of detail
- ☐ voice
- ☐ sense of story, logical sequence
- ☐ strong verbs and nouns
- ☐ strong lead, strong ending
- ☐ focus
- ☐ unity and clarity
- ☐ coherence
- ☐ character development
- ☐ effective dialogue
- ☐ literary techniques
- ☐ complex sentences

Process of Writing

- ☐ topic selection
- ☐ revision strategies/ability to revise
- ☐ ability to share writing
- ☐ use of pictures to help carry the meaning
- ☐ ability to label a picture or write a narrative
- ☐ purpose for writing
- ☐ risk-taking
- ☐ proofreading
- ☐ experimenting with different styles

Mechanics

- ☐ spelling
- ☐ punctuation
- ☐ handwriting
- ☐ paragraph breaks
- ☐ spaces
- ☐ upper/lower case
- ☐ left-to-right directionality
- ☐ grammar
- ☐ capitalization

From *The Whole Language Catalog: Forms for Authentic Assessment* © 1994 Lois Bridges Bird, Kenneth S. Goodman, and Yetta M. Goodman.

how to read, analyze, and revise my own writing. While I long for and love the response of others to my writing, I know that I'm my own best first reader.

In his book *A Fresh Look at Writing* (1994), Donald Graves reminds us that "children spend ninety-five percent of their time alone with their papers before we ever see them." So he asks, "Why not help them to improve as their own first readers?" We urge children to "write better" but we seldom give them the tools to determine if or why their writing is getting better. Thus, everything you understand about effective writing, you want to help your students understand. When students do something marvelous and surprising in their writing, celebrate it with the whole class and raise it to a level of conscious awareness. Ask the writer, "How did you do that? What were you thinking when you wrote that?" Through these writing celebrations, we help our students internalize the qualities that make their writing shine.

Next Steps

After we respond to our students' writing, we don't want to leave them hanging in a void of writing indecision. We bring our writing conferences to a successful conclusion when we take a minute or two to help the author articulate a plan about what he or she might do next. I also suggest ideas I have for next steps. Then either I or the author jots down a plan of action. The plan is not carved in stone. If the writing muse thumps authors on the head on the way back to their seats, they should feel free to forget the writing plan and follow the muse. But, more often than not, I find that a written plan of action helps writers keep up the momentum and also helps them remember

SHOPTALK

Graves, Donald H. *A Fresh Look at Writing*. Portsmouth, New Hampshire: Heinemann, 1994.

Graves gives us a fresh look at writing, with the familiar grace and humor we've come to expect of him. In his most comprehensive text on writing yet, Graves shares details on portfolios, record keeping, and methods for teaching conventions, spelling, and different genres. Throughout the text, readers will find "Actions." These are invitations to explore your own learning—to try out for yourself the writing strategies that Graves suggests. Graves' books are always a pleasure to read. *A Fresh Look at Writing* continues the tradition.

the feedback from our conference. We want our authors to leave the writing conference feeling inspired and invigorated.

For example, after Maricela and I talked about revision strategies—how to add, alter, or change information—she decided that she wanted to rewrite her account of a family fiesta as a poem. Together, we outlined how she might accomplish that. She even identified key phrases in her piece that had a poetic ring to them that could serve as starting points for a poem. By the time she returned to her desk, her writing battery was recharged and she was off and running with a new writing challenge.

The Joy of Record-Keeping

It's a teacher's worst nightmare: Thirty children are doing thirty different things, and you have lost track of them all. The reality of a writer's workshop is that you will have thirty students writing about thirty different topics. You will also have thirty students who are in different phases of the writing process—Erica is ready for the final edit of her piece, Zev is beginning a new piece while Bren and Camille are trying to revise a piece they are working on together. It's enough to make you wake up in the middle of the night in a cold sweat!

What's the solution? Keep careful records. Records are a writing teacher's best friend. A simple record-keeping system will enable you to keep track of what children are writing, of the progress they are making, and of the issues that come up in writing conferences. With this information, you are in a position to respond effectively to them each time you meet. You can also determine the pattern of writing issues in your classroom—for an individual student as well as the whole class.

For example, Javier is floundering. He continually writes in sentence fragments or run-ons. He doesn't understand how to distinguish and establish separate, complete sentences. That tells me I need to sit down with Javier and in a fifteen minute, one-on-one conference, provide him with the direct instruction he needs to learn the subtleties of sentence structure. And we'll continue to work on it. Each time I meet with Javier, I'll check his understanding of "sentenceness" and we'll keep at it until he gets it. If a fifteen-minute, one-on-one conference is an impossible luxury in your classroom, compromise—try fifteen minutes with three students who may need the same extra support, or settle for just five minutes with one student. I admit that I often spent lunch, recess, and after school time to give a needy student that extra teaching boost. It's not easy, but the extra one-on-one goes such a long way in making a difference that it's important to find a way to achieve it.

Records also help me identify the breakthroughs and writing triumphs. Tianna has done something marvelous. She has opened her new story with dialogue between the two main characters. My records show me that other students are also beginning to experiment with alternatives to "Once upon a time." I know that it's time for a whole class mini-lesson on different ways to begin a story.

It's been my experience that records work best when you design them yourself. That way you'll achieve a custom fit between your needs as a teacher, your students' needs as developing writers, and an effective record-keeping system. When designing records, simple is best. If you create something too complicated with bells and whistles and enough check-off points to confuse a computer, you'll soon abandon it. Classroom life is demanding. Record-keeping should provide comfort and relief—not additional labor! See *Assessment: Continuous Learning* (1995) in the Strategies for Teaching and Learning Professional Library for ideas about how to manage record-keeping.

It's helpful to check out other teachers' records. When designing my own, I often begin with another teacher's form and tinker with it to make it fit my unique concerns and interests. Greg Chapnick, in his chapter on Writer's Workshop, provides some helpful forms for peer conferencing, editing, and status-of-the-class reports.

Scratch the Instructional Itch

Over the years, I created mini-lessons on overhead transparencies and stored them in a loose-leaf binder. When a writing issue arose, I often had the perfect supportive mini-lesson in my binder. I was easily able to scratch my students instructionally where they were itching. I remember when Sahar made a developmental leap in her revision strategies. Instead of just adding text, the most basic sort of revision, she began to read her writing with real understanding and attempted to delete or actually rewrite text that didn't quite ring true. In my mini-lesson binder, I had several overhead transparencies that demonstrated the physical strategies writers use to revise—carets to add copy, lines to delete, arrows and carets to insert new thoughts. Sahar was burning with revision fever. I had the antidote in my binder.

This, of course, is the art of teaching. When we're able to step in at the right moment and give the writer just what they need in the way of supportive instruction, we help the writer into new realms of understanding. The Russian psychologist Lev Vygotsky (1978) defines this tension between what a child can do alone and what the child can do with assistance as the "zone of proximal development." Indeed, Vygotsky maintains that what really counts as learning is what the child is able to do with the help of an older, more experienced other, for "what a child can do with assistance today, she will be able to do by herself tomorrow."

Writers need focused instruction that will scratch them right on the spot of their writing itch. With instruction that's right on target, writers can take the writing risks that further writing development. We can't know where our students are itching instructionally, unless, over time, we observe them closely and listen carefully. We must also learn how to analyze their writing. Being an effective teacher of writing means knowing how to evaluate writing skillfully.

Let's look at how Debi Goodman, fifth-grade teacher at the Dewey Center for Urban Education in Detroit, Michigan, handles her dual role of writing teacher and writing evaluator.

SHOPTALK

Calkins, Lucy McCormick. *The Art of Teaching Writing*, New Edition. Portsmouth, New Hampshire: Heinemann, 1994.

Effective teaching, like effective writing, generally demands rethinking and revising. Not surprisingly, then, the 1994 edition of the original 1986 *The Art of Teaching Writing* is less a second edition than a whole new book. Lucy Calkins has rethought "every line and facet of [her] original text." While the content has changed, Calkins' gift for storytelling has not. A substantial 550 pages, the book is nonetheless an easy, inspiring read. And, like the original, the new edition teaches as it inspires. Teachers from preschool to high school will discover how to learn from children what to teach, how to create a viable writing workshop that supports students across the developmental continuum, how to explore multiple genres, and how to use writing to learn about the world.

My 1986 edition is tattered from use; the 1994 edition will grow old before its time for the same reason—Calkins is a masterful, compassionate teacher of writing.

See also *Living Between the Lines* (1991). Calkins and Shelley Harwayne's recommendations are simple: Narrow the gap between what professional writers do and what we expect kids to do in schools. You'll become convinced of the value of inviting students to keep writing notebooks and will want to start keeping one yourself.

Field Notes: Teacher-To-Teacher

I often have students work in partners as I give a mini-lesson on some grammatical issue. The partners proofread one person's piece for that element, then the other's. It saves my time, and they help each other develop understandings. While I'm available for questions, the partners are teaching each other, building their own language for talking about writing, pulling each other along in Vygotsky's zone of proximal development, and demonstrating the Piagetian theory that children learn best from other children. Then during conferences, I have the writers tell me about the proofreading corrections they made. I note them in my anecdotal records.

Sherry Swain
Overstreet Elementary School
Starkville, Mississippi

Lois: How do you decide what piece of writing to evaluate?

Debi: I use a writing sample from the students' regular classwork, rather than ask them to write solely for the purpose of evaluation. I prefer a writing piece that will be "published" in some way, so that I can look at the student's revision and editing strategies. I follow a simple yet thorough process.

1. I start with a revision conference with the student, looking closely at the style and quality of the writing. In such conferences, I have learned to focus on the story or report as a whole and not on specific wordings or spellings. With this focus, students will often revise by rewriting entire sections of the text, and particular wordings or spellings become unimportant for the time being.

2. I make a copy of the rough draft in order to look at it more carefully. If there are confusing passages or grammatically incorrect passages in the story, I try to determine why the writer strayed from convention. Sometimes a piece that initially seems very confusing turns out to have only one or two problems. I almost always improve my view of a student's ability by taking the time to study a piece of writing.

3. I've developed a form, "Looking Closer at a Writing Sample," that enables me to discover the writer's strengths. I keep this form in a loose-leaf binder that I use as my gradebook. It contains a divider for each child, with a sheet for reflecting on his or her writing. I place the rough draft in my gradebook so that it can be compared with previous samples. I focus my comments on the writer's capabilities and strengths.

4. After I look at the quality and style of a piece of writing, I ask the student to count the words in the first and second drafts. While longer is not always better, the number of words that a student writes indicates his or her interest in writing. If a child consistently writes very short pieces, it suggests that he or she needs some strategies for adding details and descriptions to the writing.

5. I also keep a quantitative checklist of the student's writing. Looking through the student's writing folder, I count the number of journal entries, stories, letters, and other genres the student has tried. These numbers assist me in giving the student the required letter grade in English and justifying the grade to parents and colleagues.

Looking Closer at a Writing Sample

Name _____ Date _____ Grade _____

1. To what extent is the writing clear and meaningful?

2. To what extent is it organized in an appropriate format?

3. To what extent is the writer able to present information, express a viewpoint, or tell a story?

4. To what extent is the piece interesting to read?

5. To what extent is the writer communicating with an audience in mind?

6. Is there evidence of the writer's voice?

7. Is there evidence of the writer's understanding of plot, characterization, or other literary techniques?

8. Are there some signs of beauty or brilliance?

From *The Whole Language Catalog: Forms for Authentic Assessment* © 1994 Lois Bridges Bird, Kenneth S. Goodman, and Yetta M. Goodman.

SHOPTALK

Barr, Mary. *California Learning Record: Handbook for Teachers, K-6.* Sacramento: California State Department of Education, 1993.

The California Learning Record adapted by Mary Barr from the British *Primary Language Record*, provides an excellent synthesis of developmental writing benchmarks. It helps teachers evaluate both the process of student writing as well as their polished products across genre. It includes observation forms of language across the curriculum: listening, speaking, reading, and writing. Teachers are asked to record information about their students' developing language in a variety of social and instructional contexts three times a year. *The California Learning Record* provides teachers with detailed theoretical information about language and learning, how to record and interpret it, and how to develop instructional and curriculum strategies to extend and refine their students' understanding. I highly recommend it.

Use your knowledge of writing together with the qualities of effective writing you consider important to create the rubric.

What about Rubrics?

As educators move away from letter grades, many are adopting developmental rubrics instead. While it may be tempting to use the rubric as a checklist of completed items, rubrics are most helpful when they are used as a guide to quality. Use your knowledge of writing together with the qualities of effective writing you consider important to create the rubric. Look at what other teachers have done and adapt their ideas to fit your own needs. Then help your students aim for the content standards of the rubric as they write. I recommend that you post the rubric in the room or give every student a copy of it. Talk about the rubric frequently. Invite students to evaluate their own writing and determine where they might place themselves on the rubric. Students need to understand what to aim for as they work to become more skillful writers.

Evaluate the Writing Self

We want our students to become the best first readers of their own writing. That means they have to know how to evaluate their writing selves. Mary Kitagawa teaches a fifth-sixth grade combination at Mark's Meadow School in Amherst, Massachusetts. She has designed "Survey in the Language Arts: Writing" that she asks her students to complete twice a year, once at the beginning and again toward the end of school. She also fills out the survey on

Survey in the Language Arts: Writing

Observational Rating   Self   Teacher
In each set, mark the sentence that best describes you as a writer.   (circle one)

Fluency
☐ I usually find it easy to express my ideas in writing.
☐ I sometimes find it easy to express my ideas in writing.
☐ I often find it hard to write, but I keep at it anyway.
☐ I have to struggle to write anything, so I never enjoy it.

Topic choice
☐ I easily come up with a wide variety of possible topics.
☐ I frequently find topics without much difficulty.
☐ I am usually surprised and relieved when I find a good topic.
☐ I can never come up with good topics, so I just write on any old topic.

Voice
☐ I deliberately let my own "voice" come through, if appropriate.
☐ I often find my own "voice" coming through in many of my texts.
☐ I am becoming aware of my own "voice," especially in journals.
☐ I do not know what my own "voice" is.

Genre
☐ I write poetry, fiction, personal narratives, essays, reports, letters, reading logs, etc.
☐ I am learning to write in most of the above genres.
☐ I write in several of the above genres; I am willing to try any of them.
☐ I don't feel I can write in most of the above ways.

Deadlines, portfolios, and journal/notebook requirements
☐ I easily surpass all requirements on time or am often early.
☐ I meet all requirements without reminders.
☐ I meet the minimal requirements when I am given reminders of a specially set-aside time to accomplish them.
☐ I do not fulfill requirements or follow organizational procedures.

Writing process
☐ I decide for myself when and how to draft, revise, edit, or use strategies such as free-writing, brainstorming, etc.
☐ I am usually able to make use of the processes listed above.
  I use the processes above with help and guidance.
☐ I expect an adult to tell me what to do next in writing.

Proofreading and editing
☐ I am successful and reliable in proofreading and editing.
☐ I am working on proofreading and editing skills.
☐ I can proofread and edit, but I often forget or fail to do so.
☐ I don't proofread or edit unless someone makes me do it.

Other information about yourself as a writer:

From *The Whole Language Catalog: Forms for Authentic Assessment* © 1994 Lois Bridges Bird, Kenneth S. Goodman, and Yetta M. Goodman.

each student and then compares her analysis to the student's self-analysis. The first descriptors indicate great confidence. The last ones suggest a sense of inadequacy and difficulty seeing through a writing project to successful completion. Mary explains how she uses the survey.

> Most students select descriptors from the middle of these two extremes, which differ primarily in degree of success and diligence, although both reflect functional involvement with writing and reasonable participation in writing workshop. If a student marks many of the last choices, I would earmark that student for some confidence building. I have not been surprised when fluent and competent students mark themselves less so, especially in writing. Experienced writers know how complex a task it is. A large measure of their motivation comes from untangling and reweaving those wonderful, terrible complexities. The more writers know about writing, the less likely they are to glibly consider themselves masters of it.

Surrounded by forms and checklists and rubrics, we may forget the easiest step of all. Just ask your students to list out what they know about writing. Mary, Tim, Tonin, Delano, Caryn, and Larry, fifth graders in Rena Malkofsky's classroom at El Carmelo School in Palo Alto, California, composed such a list and suggested that Rena pass it on to her new fifth graders next year to give them a jump start on writing.

Assess To Teach

Rich documentation of students' writing helps us in our role as writing teachers in two important ways. One, it enables us to share our students' writing development with their parents. There is perhaps no more valuable evaluation tool than a writing folder brimming with writing of all sorts, our evaluation of each piece, and the author's self-evaluative comments. Parents are treated to a multifaceted view of their budding author. At the same time, the writing folder and our analysis of it show us exactly what instruction the budding author needs in order to bloom.

When looking at the work of a developing writer, our eyes may glaze over as we're accosted by misspelled words, misplaced modifiers, and misleading logic. Avoid the impulse to teach it all. Indeed, effective teaching demands restraint. Identify one or two salient points and teach those well. In other words, young authors can't learn how to handle topic focus, theme, voice, commas, semicolons, and paragraph breaks all in one day. But they probably can tackle one or two of those issues, return to their pieces and work diligently to improve them with those two issues in mind. With their next piece, they'll be responsible for handling those two issues plus two more that you identify from your assessment records. Eventually, by the end of the year, they'll have refined their control over and understanding of a wide spectrum of writing issues. So be patient and don't stuff too much teaching into just

Field Notes: Teacher-To-Teacher

It's a great idea to have students who learn a specific technique become the house expert on it. That way more students can be reached without driving you nuts. For example, when Xavier learned how to handle quotation marks to designate dialogue, he became our "quotation mark expert." As other children began using dialogue in their compositions, I would refer them to Xavier who would explain how to set dialogue apart with indentation and punctuation. It saved me valuable time, was a real ego-boost for Xavier, and proved to the children that in our room, everyone is both a teacher and a learner.

Greg Chapnick
Charquin School
Hayward, California

one conference. And to help you and your slowly blooming authors keep track of what they know and what they still need to know, ask them to keep another form stapled to their folder that lists the skills and understandings they've mastered.

Be Yourself

A final note about how to respond to young writers—be yourself. Always listen first as a caring, compassionate human being. Let the writing teacher in you emerge when it's appropriate.

When we invite our students to choose writing topics they care about, they may pull material deep from within troubled places in their lives. It's important to consider how you feel about receiving such material in your classroom. You may want to discuss it with your students, and, depending on their ages, solicit their opinions. Jason Cetron is a second grader at Curtis Estabrook School in Brooklyn, New York. His teacher, Maureen Powell, sent me Jason's thoughts about writing as therapy. "Keep writing, keep crying," Jason advises us. "When you write you might write something sad, and you might start crying. Ignore the crying, and keep writing. If you can't ignore the crying, just keep writing and cry at the same time."

When we invite our students to choose writing topics they care about, they may pull material deep from within troubled places in their lives.

The Chinese came here to get rich but they were treat unequally because they Californians thought they were different and weird.

Third-grade teacher Sara Mosle, in her moving *New Yorker* article, "Writing Down Secrets," (1995) describes how when one boy's uncle died, she made the mistake of asking him, "Are you sad?" The boy wrote back to her in his journal: "Why would you ask a question like that? You make me sadder because my uncle is dead. I'll get over it. Don't remind me anymore, please? I loved him so much."

You may want to establish guidelines distinguishing private writing from public writing. You'll also want to establish careful guidelines for receiving sensitive material. Honest writing bares one's soul. Sharing personal writing is an act of courage. Children should always enter a sharing period with a sense of sacredness, ready to listen hard to the writer and to respond, first of all, as caring, compassionate human beings.

SHOPTALK

Hindley, Joanne. *In the Company of Children.* York, Maine: Stenhouse Publishers, 1996.

Hindley writes with conviction because she loves the company of children. And in their company as their teacher, she has developed sensitive and deeply thoughtful ways to support and foster their literacy development. Clearly a talented educator, Hindley shares her strategies for

- launching writer's notebooks
- helping students move from their notebooks to more formal projects
- keeping records to guide mini-lessons
- inspiring sensitive responses to literature
- assessing student progress.

Hindley's book is a pleasure to read. Everything she writes rings true because you know that she has done it herself—all in the company of thirty-some diverse students.

Chapter 5

The Conventions Writers and Readers Need

There is a time and place for convention, and it's not at the first rush of creativity in a first draft as students concentrate on carving out their meaning. Indeed, young writers may lose their meaning if they have to stop the flow of composing to "get it right." Concern with correctness and convention comes in later drafts as students polish and refine their meaning.

In the writer's workshops I've enjoyed with young people, we follow this general plan of writing-revising-editing action as outlined by such experts as Graves (1983), Atwell (1987), and Calkins (1986, 1991). Let's follow Daniella through the process.

First draft. Daniella focuses on finding her meaning. What is she trying to say? She pays little attention to the "road signs" of correct spelling and punctuation. As an older, more experienced writer, Daniella tends to write even first drafts in a conventional manner. Checking her spelling and noting commas, however, is not her primary concern as she's absorbed in creating her message.

Subsequent drafts. Daniella continues to tinker with her meaning, fine-tuning her word choice, adjusting her sentence structure, and in general concentrating on refining the ways in which she has expressed herself.

Final draft. Using an editing checklist and a blue pencil, Daniella checks for her departures from convention. She corrects as many as she can.

Daniella's edited draft. She turns it into the editor-in-chief (me). I review and edit with a green pencil. I also note in my assessment records the writing hurdles Daniella has cleared (strengths) as well as her stumbles (needs). I choose one or two needs to focus on in our editing conference and I teach her what she needs to know in order to avoid those pitfalls in her subsequent writing.

Further edits. With her new understandings, she returns to her piece, corrects the problems we discussed, and turns the piece back to me for my final edit.

Publishing. If it's a piece we've both deemed worthy of "publishing," she types in the final corrections on the computer or gives it to a parent-helper who has volunteered to type up student writing for us at home.

You may notice that I didn't number these writing process steps. That's because writing is not a linear process. All writers follow their own idiosyncratic composing paths and retrace their steps at different times. I tend to compose one paragraph at a time—sometimes one sentence—and then cycle back again and again to refine my meaning. It's hard for me to press on with new thoughts until what I already have down on paper rings true.

DIALOGUE

How do I compose—in a great creative charge or slowly, one careful word at a time?

_____

_____

At what point do I begin to revise—after I have a complete first draft or simultaneously as I compose?

_____

_____

At what point in my own writing do I become concerned with conventional spelling, punctuation, and grammar?

_____

_____

At what point do I feel comfortable sharing my writing with others and receiving their feedback?

_____

_____

The art of the writing teacher is to focus on the writer's strengths—celebrate all that the writer can do—and then nudge the writer forward with sensitive instruction delivered at the point of need.

Understanding Development

It may be true that there are as many writing processes as there are writers. Certainly, age and experience affect the writing process. In my unbiased opinion, my second grade son, Brennan, shows promise as a developing writer. However, the process he follows as a seven year old does not parallel the writing process of a Toni Morrison or even his fourteen-year-old sister, Aislinn.

As teachers of writing, we cannot expect the same of every student. And we most certainly have to consider the developmental age and ability of every writer with whom we work. What we expect of our first grade writers differs qualitatively from our expectations for our third grade writers. The art of the writing teacher is to focus on the writer's strengths—celebrate all that the writer can do—and then nudge the writer forward with sensitive instruction delivered at the point of need.

As we plan instruction for our young writers, we must also understand how written language develops and how children acquire the conventions that help readers. Piaget, the great Swiss psychologist, helped us understand that learning is a very active process. Children work and play hard to make sense of their world. The same active construction that children engage in as they learn about the world also governs their exploration of language. Children quite literally invent their way into language. Those of us who have been around young children just learning to talk know how charming the results can be. "Look, Ma," shouted one youngster, skipping out the door and stripping down to his naked self, "I'm barefoot all over!" (Chukovskii 1968).

As children have more extensive encounters with the real world, they become increasingly aware of the conventions that govern language. Gradually, as they work to achieve equilibrium between their views of the world and the real world, they modify their inventions and learn the conventions.

SHOPTALK

Bissex, Glenda L. *GNYS AT WRK: A Child Learns to Write and Read.* Cambridge, Massachusetts: Harvard University Press, 1980.

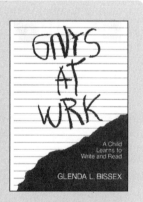

For a fascinating account of one child's journey into the conventional world of written language, read Glenda Bissex's *GNYS AT WRK.* Bissex traces the development of her son, Paul, from the ages of five to ten, as he grows into an accomplished reader and writer. As we follow the twists and turns, stops and spurts, in Paul's literacy journey, we gain insight into the developmental linguistic odysseys of all children. What was true for Paul can be true for all children provided we, like Bissex, invite them to explore literacy, and then trust and respect them as learners.

SHOPTALK

Dyson, Anne Hass. *Multiple Worlds of Child Writers: Friends Learning to Write.* New York: Teachers College Press, 1989.

Oakland, California, teacher Pam Bovyer Cook says of this book, "Anne Hass Dyson, professor of language and literacy at the Graduate School of Education, University of California, Berkeley, is a former classroom teacher and now project director in emergent literacy for the Center for the Study of Writing. Her research in this study focuses on children's oral and written language use in the classroom. This book, one of several she has written, is a study of the emerging literacy of five first graders with diverse social and ethnic backgrounds in an urban school. It focuses on the peer group and classroom context as supports for developing writers. Dyson wonderfully captures the classroom community the children and their teacher create—a community which is supported by and supportive of the children's growth as writers. Dyson clearly demonstrates that if children are to develop as writers, their stories must be connected to their social and personal lives. As the book progresses…'the children grow as writers of imagined worlds, and that growth is linked to their lives together as friends and scholars, as fellow reflectors in the world they share.'"

Learning a language— oral or written—is a developmental process.

Learning a language—oral or written—is a developmental process. You may ask, "If language learning is developmental, then what role do I, as the teacher, play? Is there even a role for me?" Absolutely! We're not suggesting that you create a classroom garden of print, plant your students, and then retreat behind the garden gate while you wait for them to blossom into readers and writers. The art of teaching requires sensitive mediation at the point of need. We have a critical role in helping our students come to understand the conventions that govern language and the ways in which those conventions help writers convey meaning. Let's look at how primary writers acquire the skills and conventions that will support their writing. Over the years, I've come across many frameworks that explain the developmental course of orthographic knowledge. I find one that Constance Weaver shares in her book *Reading Process and Practice: From Socio-Psycholinguistics to Whole Language* (1988) particularly helpful. You can use a framework such as the one that follows to ascertain your students' developmental understanding of spelling.

Developmental Phases of Spelling

Pre-phonetic (pretend writing). As children attempt to spell words, they write what appear to be random letter strings. Children in this phase display no visible awareness of sound-letter correspondence. What is their spelling strat-egy? To spell a word, children jot down some letters. Often the letters children write are the ones they're most familiar with, those from their own name. The longer children think the word is, the more letters they write. Take a look at the example below from my daughter Erin.

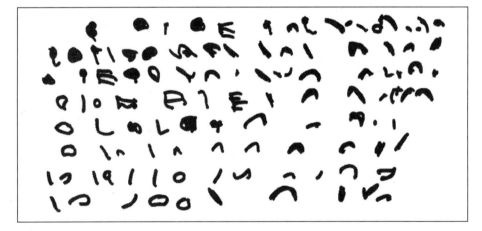

Phonetic. Children in the phonetic phase are aware of sound-letter relation-ships and they tend to represent that relationship in a predictable order. First, they write initial consonants only; secondly, initial and final consonants;

third, long vowels that "say their names;" and finally, short vowels. So, to spell a word, you write the initial consonants only [D for dog]; later you add final consonants [DG]; and only later do you begin to hear and add vowel sounds as well.

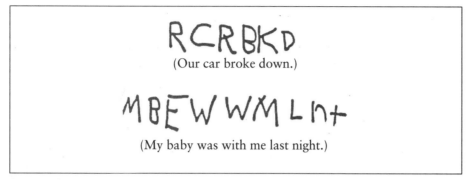

RCRBKD
(Our car broke down.)

MBEWWMLnt
(My baby was with me last night.)

From Temple, C., Nathan, R., Burris, N.A. *The Beginnings of Writing*, Third Edition © 1993 by Allyn and Bacon. Reprinted by permission.

Letter name. Children in the letter name phase write letters for at least three of the sounds they hear. As in the example I've provided, the letters include vowels (particularly those that "say their names") as well as consonants.

GRENIMbXI.

(Jewelry in my box.)

Transitional. Once children reach the transitional phase, they are moving away from a strict phonetic strategy and are relying on their visual memory of having seen words in print. They also can rely on their beginning understanding of the orthographic system. In this phase, to spell a word, children use what they remember from seeing the word in print. If they don't remember how a word is spelled, they can try to use the "rules" for spelling they've observed in print (e.g., final e to make a preceding vowel long).

Elaine

At my house i have some dayseses they are flowrs they growe in the spreing i pike them in the spreing the rain mak the flowrs growe and in the somre they all droy up and more lowrs growe bak and they have naw levs and i poke them agan.

From Temple, C., Nathan, R., Burris, N.A. *The Beginnings of Writing*, Third Edition © 1993 by Allyn and Bacon. Reprinted by permission.

As you work with young writers, it's most helpful to engage them in self-evaluation of their own spelling strategies. Try self-reflective questions such as these. I think you'll find the information you receive quite informative.

- What words do you think you've spelled correctly? Will you circle them for me?
- Which ones aren't you sure about? Will you underline them?
- Why did you decide on this particular spelling?
- How else could you spell this word?
- If this word is incorrect, how could you find the correct spelling?

As students participate in lively discussions about spelling strategies, they learn to analyze and articulate their own strategies. Additionally, they absorb helpful strategies suggested by their classmates. Here's a list of spelling strategies some first-grade friends of mine have shared with me over the years.

How To Spell a Word

- Stretch the word out like a rubber band in your mouth and listen to all the sounds you hear. Write the sounds down. (See Calkins' *The Art of Teaching Writing*, for her discussion of this strategy.)
- Ask a friend who is a good speller.
- Look around the room and see if you see the word spelled somewhere. (Donald Graves, in his book *Writing: Teachers and Children at Work*, refers to this as "living off the land." Children scan the classroom print for words they want to spell.)
- Remember seeing the word in a book; look it up. (I've actually watched children leave their desks, pull a book from a shelf, flip open to a specific page, and copy a word they had remembered seeing in the book.)
- Write the word three different ways. Choose the spelling that "looks right."
- Try to use the dictionary.
- Use the spell-checker on the computer.

These are all excellent ways to figure out an unknown spelling. I use them myself. How about you? What are your spelling strategies?

Talk about Writing

As often as possible, invite children to describe how and why they made the decisions they did as writers. This includes decisions about all aspects of

As you work with young writers, it's most helpful to engage them in self-evaluation of their own spelling strategies.

SHOPTALK

Newman, Judith. *The Craft of Children's Writing*. Portsmouth, New Hampshire: Heinemann, 1984.

Newman leads readers through the multiple dimensions of written language development using striking samples of children's writing, including an in-depth case study of six-year-old Shawn. A slim text simply organized around the four developmental concepts of intention, organization, experimentation, and orchestration, it's a good book to hand parents or teachers unfamiliar with literacy as a developmental language process.

writing, everything from handling writing conventions to choosing topics to using illustrations to support their writing. By talking about writing, we enable students to hold it up to the light of self-analysis and examine what they know about it, what they are learning, and what they still need to know. Questions we might ask include, "How did you decide to write about your conversation with a homeless man? Why did you begin with a flashback? Describing summer as a bird on wing is a wonderful metaphor…how did you think of it? I see you've used dashes here to separate this phrase—how did you think of that? What do you think you accomplish by setting the phrase off with dashes?"

When we ask children to explain how and why, we begin from a position of trust. We trust that our young writers have lots of important knowledge about written language and that they are using their knowledge—often in wonderfully creative, unique ways—to write and make sense of their world. Talking with kids about such conventional concerns as spelling, punctuation, and grammar accomplishes yet another important goal. It helps kids learn that such conventions matter. Make no mistake about it—correct spelling, punctuation, and grammar count. While it's true we don't need to worry about them when we're swept up in the heat of composing, conventions become important as we cool down and begin to look at our writing with a critical eye. We step back from our second, third, or fourth drafts and try to read our text through the eyes of our potential readers. We tinker with our text, correct misspelled words, add missing punctuation, and eliminate clutter (unnecessary words) to make our text as reader-friendly as possible.

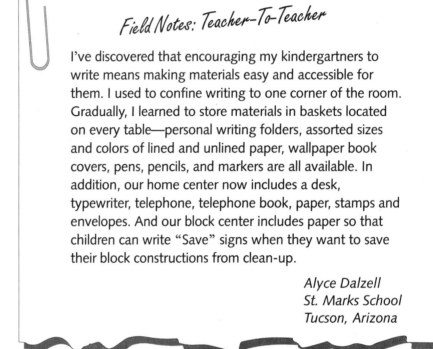

Field Notes: Teacher-To-Teacher

I've discovered that encouraging my kindergartners to write means making materials easy and accessible for them. I used to confine writing to one corner of the room. Gradually, I learned to store materials in baskets located on every table—personal writing folders, assorted sizes and colors of lined and unlined paper, wallpaper book covers, pens, pencils, and markers are all available. In addition, our home center now includes a desk, typewriter, telephone, telephone book, paper, stamps and envelopes. And our block center includes paper so that children can write "Save" signs when they want to save their block constructions from clean-up.

Alyce Dalzell
St. Marks School
Tucson, Arizona

Jason Cetron, an eight year old in Maureen Powell's second-grade class in Curtis Estabrook School in Brooklyn, understands the value of punctuation.

> Punctuation and capitalization are very important. If you don't use them, it will be very hard to read your sentences. I'll show you what I mean. once there was a lady she had sheep goats and chickens she loved them very much one day she had a baby she loved the baby more than the animals Do you see what I mean? Punctuation and capitalization are very, very important.

What about Skills?

I hope this discussion has helped you deal with that most difficult question, "What about skills?" Skills make sense and are easy to learn when you have a reason to need them. When Daniella introduces dialogue in her mystery story, I know it's time to pull her aside and do a mini-lesson on the ways writers use quotation marks and indentation to introduce dialogue. We don't leave skills to chance. We teach them within the context of the child's writing. We respond to what the child is trying to do, and we add to their repertoire of skills as we deem appropriate.

There's another reason to teach skills within the context of students' own writing—it's more effective and efficient. Instead of handing out the same skills worksheets year after year and finding out that kids still don't know how to use a comma, we teach the skills as our students need to use them in their own writing. For those of you who quake at the thought of giving up your skills worksheets, let me share a reassuring story with you.

Lucy Calkins, who directs the Writer's Project at Teacher's College in New York City, spent two years as Donald Graves' research assistant studying the writing development of elementary school children at Atkinson Academy in Durham, New Hampshire. Calkins (1983) conducted her own independent mini-research on the issue of how best to teach punctuation. She interviewed students from two third-grade classrooms. Mrs. West taught a traditional regimen of skills and drill. "She often wrote sentences on the chalkboard and asked her children to insert the missing punctuation," Calkins explains. Mrs. West "made dittos on question marks, and gave tests before and after each lesson. Her children rarely wrote and when they did, Mrs. West vigilantly re-penned each error." In Pat Howard's classroom, the children participated in a writer's workshop. They learned skills as they were editing their own writing.

Calkins asked children from the two classrooms to tell her what each punctuation mark meant and how it was used. She found that the youngsters in Pat Howard's classroom could explain an average of more than eight kinds of punctuation. The children from Mrs. West's room, on the other hand, "who had studied punctuation through classwork, drills and tests, but had rarely written, were able to explain fewer than four kinds." Even more striking was the way in which the children from the two classrooms defined punctuation. Mrs. West's students had trouble explaining what the

S H O P T A L K

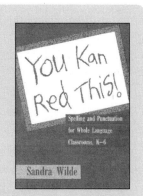

Wilde, Sandra. *You Kan Red This! Spelling and Punctuation for Whole Language Classrooms, K-6.* Portsmouth, New Hampshire: Heinemann, 1992.

My friend and colleague, Sandra Wilde, has written the widely-acclaimed book, *You Kan Red This!* Wilde explains that children's invented spellings are not random; indeed, they reflect sophisticated patterns that represent the children's developing understanding of the orthographic system. Wilde shows you how to analyze children's inventions, identify patterns, and use the patterns to determine what children understand about spelling. With that information, you can design instruction that will help your students become more effective spellers.

DIALOGUE

How have I handled writing skills instruction?

_____

_____

_____

If I've relied on skills work, would I be willing to turn instead
to teaching skills within the context of my students' writing?
Why or why not?

_____

_____

_____

If I have taught skills within the context of my students' writing, what have I noticed about their use of and understanding
of skills?

_____

_____

_____

Parents are understandably concerned that their children
acquire needed skills. How can I help parents understand the
ways in which I address skills?

_____

_____

_____

---

punctuation was for; one youngster described commas as "those things you
stick between fruit." Can you guess how he came up with that definition?
Remember the worksheets? In contrast, Pat Howard's students had acquired
a functional understanding of how each kind of punctuation supported their
writing. Listen to Wendy's explanation of commas: "Before and after the
comma, they are parts of the same sentence. Like the first half of the sentence
is one paragraph, and the other half is the second paragraph like two edges
of the same idea. It seems clear, then, that skill-teaching is most effective
within the context of real writing. But what skills should you teach? Pam

Bovyer Cook answers, "The skills I teach change every year." That's because Bovyer Cook is sensitive to the unique needs and interests of each class of students she works with and responds accordingly. Here's a list of the writing skills she's working on this year with her current class:

- personification
- sensory images
- similes and metaphors
- balance of dialogue and narrative
- other ways of saying "said"
- big (climaxing) event
- historical facts (handling of historical detail).

Rena Malkofsky routinely asks her fifth-grade students to self-evaluate. "What do you know about writing? List it out." Amy lists her knowledge about commas. Amy is clearly a comma-expert. Indeed, she's earned that reputation in her classroom and when others need help evaluating the placement of a comma, they know who to go to for help.

Commas   Amy

1. I use commas to separate a list of things.
   I like apples, pears, plums and grapes.
2. I use commas to separate citrus + states
   I live in Palo Alto, CA.
3. I use a comma to separate unecessary information.
   Rena, my teacher, was sick last week.
4. I use commas to separate an exclamation.
   Wow, what great earrings you have!
5. I use commas to separate time.
   Yesterday, I went to the store.

A quick note about how to handle the logistics of instruction. First of all, make sure that your students understand that there are thirty learners in the classroom—and thirty writing teachers. Your students should know that they can go to each other for help. Also, make good use of your time. Whenever possible, arrange to teach specific skills to several students at a time. Let's say that you have a list of fifty skills. Fifty times thirty students equals 1,500 individual skill lessons and that equals impossible. Teaching a skill at the point of need (versus because you are on page 24 of the Language Arts textbook) is the most effective way to teach, but you have to be smart about managing your time.

The questions you ask children today are the questions they can ask on their own tomorrow.

SHOPTALK

Calkins, Lucy McCormick. *Lessons from a Child: On the Teaching and Learning of Writing*. Portsmouth, New Hampshire: Heinemann, 1983.

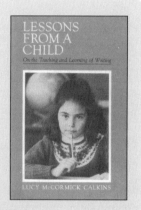

Here's a professional book that reads like a novel. As we follow one child's growth in writing, we learn about written language development, in general, as well as how to organize our classrooms for writing. Matters of classroom management, methods for helping children use the peer conference, and ways in which mini-lessons can extend children's understanding of good writing are all woven into this dramatic tale of one child and of her classroom at Atkinson Elementary School in New Hampshire.

We can have confidence that our students will acquire the skills they need if we follow these practices:

- We invite students to write, write, write, and use the conventions in their writing.
- We provide direct instruction at the point of need, being sensitive to the ways in which written language develops.
- We demonstrate the use of conventions in our own writing and point out the conventions in the work of published authors.
- We discuss the importance of conventions with our students and invite them to share their strategies for dealing with them.
- We ask children questions that enable students to self-reflect and monitor their own use of conventions.

The questions you ask children today are the questions they can ask on their own tomorrow. Our ultimate goal is to help children control all the many decisions they face as they create a written composition. When children can ask questions of themselves and of their writing and know how to answer them, they are on their way to becoming skilled writers.

Chapter 6

Write Your Way into Learning

In fourth grade, American school children dig into their state's history. As a fourth grader, I attended University Hill Elementary, a three-story, red brick schoolhouse built on a rocky hill across the street from the University of Colorado. The physical history of Colorado was all around us, but we never ventured outside nor turned the corner to walk five short blocks to Boulder's Historical Museum. We turned the pages of our social studies textbook, instead. We read about the geography, the agriculture, the history, and the industry of Colorado. Then our teacher, Mrs. Warren, gave us our assignment—to write a report about Colorado. I can't remember anything I wrote. That's probably because I dug my words right out of the *World Book Encyclopedia* that we kept neatly lined on a bookshelf at home. No one ever taught me how to mine gems of information from multiple sources nor how to jot down notes in my own words, choose a focused topic, and craft an original text.

School research is a peculiar beast—quite unlike anything that passes for the exciting stuff of real-life inquiry. I'm reminded of James Herndon's (1971) wry observation of flax, "I think you could live your entire life in America and never see or even hear of flax, never know about it or need to know about it," Herndon muses. "Only in school, only from the geography textbook, only from the teacher could you learn about flax."

SHOPTALK

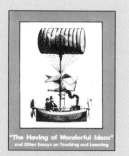

Duckworth, Eleanor. *The Having of Wonderful Ideas and Other Essays on Teaching and Learning.* New York: Teachers College Press, 1987.

Sandra Wilde of Portland State University says of Duckworth's book, "This may be one of the best books about teaching and learning ever written." In a variety of fascinating essays about topics such as children making bulbs light up and teachers observing the moon and thinking about what they see, Duckworth offers a distinctly Piagetian perspective on how we come to know, and on the role schools play in that knowing. Duckworth combines a strong background in Piaget (she worked with him and was one of his translators) with probing intelligence that is never content to take things for granted. Every page contains interesting revelations and insights. The main message: it is absolutely imperative for learners to invent the wheel, for it is through invention rather than transmission that true learning occurs.

When we consider student research, we need to explore the ways in which we can help children discover their own ideas and define their own questions.

"The Having of Wonderful Ideas"

The students at Fair Oaks School in Redwood City, California, do know how to think and write in their own words. Indeed, they understand how to ask their own questions. And although they love books and printed information of all sorts, they also know that sometimes the best source of information is another human being. Fair Oaks has a tradition of organizing curriculum around student inquiry, and, as a result, students quickly grow into independent research and thinking.

Once, during a discussion with nine-year-old Karla Sandoval, I asked her what she liked best about Fair Oaks. She thought long and hard before answering, but when she found the words she wanted, I felt my pulse quicken. Karla said, "At other schools, they teach you about other people's ideas; at Fair Oaks, they help you discover your own ideas."

Karla's understanding sets the theme for this chapter. Children do have big ideas, big questions, and big concerns about the world—ideas, questions, and concerns that we need to value, respect, and support in the classroom. When we consider student research, we need to explore the ways in which we can help children discover their own ideas and define their own questions.

Pam Bovyer Cook reminds us of another critical reason to listen to and embrace students' questions, ideas, and concerns. "In the inner city," Bovyer

Cook writes, "students experience traumas that need to be dealt with, discussed, and problem solved in the classroom. When these traumas are not acknowledged, the result is school failure, alienation, and ultimately students who feel compelled to drop out." Student inquiry is a way to help these kids take control of their lives and to find positive solutions to complex problems.

What Have You Always Wondered About?

There are many ways to get students started on research, to help them identify questions that will guide their inquiry. Perhaps the easiest is simply to ask, "What have you always wondered about? What have you always wanted to know, but have never had the opportunity to find out?" (And who knows, some day you may encounter a student who says, "Flax!")

In this way, students can consider the mysteries of life over which they have puzzled: "Why are stoplights yellow, green, and red?" "Why do bats hang upside down?" "What is it like to be an identical twin?" After recording a list of all their musings, they can debate and negotiate which topic might work best to pursue in a whole-class research project. Students can also work independently. Those who are experienced researchers may prefer to conduct independent research and explore their own questions. Some teachers invite students to do both. They involve their students in a class research project that satisfies curriculum guidelines and, at the same time, invite them to pursue independent research projects around personal topics of interest. One year, in Leslie Mangiola's fifth-sixth grade class at Fair Oaks, independent student researchers hunted down the facts on everything from manatees to rock star promoters.

Field Notes: Teacher-To-Teacher

Last year, some of my students found an interesting twist on the traditional autobiography. We kept reading and writing portfolios throughout the year. The only stipulation I gave was that anything in the portfolio needed to somehow reflect the student as a reader or writer. Several students wanted to include family photos, so they wrote about how their families influenced them as writers and readers. This idea caught on quickly, and soon many students were following up on it.

Rena Malkofsky
El Carmelo School
Palo Alto, California

SHOPTALK

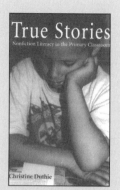

Duthie, Christine. *True Stories: Nonfiction Literacy in the Primary Classroom.* York, Maine: Stenhouse Publishers, 1996.

If you ever doubted that young children are capable of understanding and creating nonfiction materials, your doubts will vanish as you read Christine Duthie's remarkable *True Stories*. I found myself stopping on nearly every page to record in my notebook one profound idea after another for conducting nonfiction author studies, using nonfiction in reading and writing workshops, and reading and writing biography and autobiography. In Duthie, we have a wise guide, indeed, to the world of nonfiction literacy, a world we seldom invite young children to enter. With this book on your nightstand (yes, it's good enough for bedtime reading), you'll know how to enter this world and take your students with you. And Duthie's book most certainly won't remain on your nightstand—it's far too valuable to be anywhere but in your hands, offering inspiration and marvelous ideas for nurturing children's natural curiosity about the world. *True Stories* is a true delight.

A multimedia blitz. For one week, turn your classroom into a Multimedia Learning Fair. Choose a theme and then "blitz" your students with everything you can get your hands on related to the theme—written material of all sorts including children's literature, poetry, plays, magazines, newspapers, and written documents. And don't forget audiotapes of music, videotapes, filmstrips, photographs, hands-on artifacts, and the like. Over the course of a week or two, as children explore this material, they'll make connections and ask questions which then become the starting point for a research project.

Explore the textbook. In the context of having wonderful ideas, let's consider the worst-case scenario—a textbook that you are required to teach cover to cover. If you can help students forge a meaningful learning path into this textbook and find writing topics that matter to them, then all other writing challenges that come your way will be easy. First, you don't need to cover the textbook; let the kids do that. Here's how—mentally divide the textbook into chunks or sections that your students can reasonably manage. Perhaps you want to go chapter by chapter or combine chapters into larger sections. Once you've decided on a reasonable chunk, ask the students to read it and to keep track of things that interest them or questions that arise as they are reading it. They can use self-stick notes to mark passages of interest or jot down notes and questions in a reading log.

Once they've spent time in small groups reading, discussing, and musing over the textbook chunk, pull them together in a large group and list out what they found. It's been my experience that there's always lots of overlap in what students identify as interesting or worthy of further study.

Together, find ways to combine and organize their questions so that you whittle it down to about five overarching questions. These will serve as the guiding questions for the next several weeks. Your students will need to choose one question that they want to pursue further, so if you have five questions, you'll have five research groups. The textbook is one reference. Students investigate a variety of informational sources. Not every student studies every page of the textbook. Before you accuse me of breaking the teaching commandment, "Thou shalt cover the curriculum," let me suggest a more meaningful goal—uncover the curriculum through student research.

Uncovering the curriculum means that students delve deeper into the textbook through their own research. They use their own genuine questions as research guides and search the textbook as well as other materials for answers. The result? Students ultimately achieve an understanding of the material that far transcends the usual surface skimming they do when they have to read the text cover to cover. As each small research group completes their investigations, they share their findings with the whole class in a formal research

Uncovering the curriculum means that students delve deeper into the textbook through their own research.

SHOPTALK

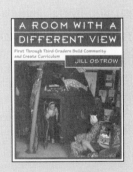

Ostrow, Jill. *A Room with a Different View: First Through Third Graders Build Community and Create Curriculum.* York, Maine: Stenhouse Publishers, 1995.

Imagine turning your classroom into a tropical island! That's exactly what Jill Ostrow and her six- to nine-year-old students did. Along the way, they negotiated curriculum, worked in collaborative groups, and used all the content areas to solve real-world problems. They kept journals of their trips to other countries, drew up lists of materials and resources they needed, researched holidays in other countries and cultures, and in general used writing continually as a tool to guide their learning. You might not care to transform your classroom physically, but read this delightful book and you'll discover ways you can transform your curriculum to create a true learner-centered community where children are able to explore their learning passions.

presentation. So, while students are uncovering the curriculum, they are also covering it. Every student eventually receives information about the range of topics contained in the textbook.

A Learning Framework

Once your students have identified a research topic, you'll want to introduce them to the framework for independent research. If you are currently using the Galef Institute's *Different Ways of Knowing* curriculum modules, then you'll be familiar with its four-step model that parallels the natural process of human learning. The four "wheels" provide a very helpful framework for independent student research. Let's review them briefly.

S H O P T A L K

Steffey, Stephanie and Wendy J. Hood, eds. *If This Is Social Studies, Why Isn't It Boring?* York, Maine: Stenhouse Publishers, 1994.

Follow the ideas and strategies in this book (almost all from practicing classroom teachers) and your students won't expect social studies to be boring ever again. Teachers from elementary to high school will find diverse ways to transcend the social studies textbook. Literature studies, theme cycles, student inquiry, critical pedagogy, and storytelling are some of the tools the chapter authors use to help their students ask powerful questions, tackle difficult issues, research multiple resources, and find answers that stimulate new questions. The authors explore contemporary subjects such as the Gulf War, traditional subjects such as students as historians, and timely issues such as multiculturalism.

Wheel 1: Exploring what you already know. Our children have been on the planet for five, six, seven, or more years. They already know a lot about our world. Begin with that knowledge. In Wheel 1, students discover and show what they already know about their chosen research question or theme. Their prior knowledge motivates them to cross the conceptual bridge to further exploration of the big idea or theme.

Wheel 2: Getting smarter through research. Here's their chance to do real research. Immerse them in all sorts of exciting materials. In Wheel 2, students gather information as they search for answers to their guiding questions.

Wheel 3: Becoming an expert. In Wheel 3, students collate their research findings, pull everything together, write it up, and find a way to share with others what they've learned. Do discourage "This-Is-What-I-Learned" reports. Encourage novel and challenging ways to showcase learning—how about a musical revue? a video production? a poster exhibit?

Wheel 4: Making connections to lifelong learning. Learning is a process of making connections, of understanding how things are related. As reflective learners, children connect what they're learning to their own lives. When we ask thoughtful questions, we help children synthesize their new knowledge and apply it to new situations. One line of inquiry leads to another.

Once the children have their guiding question and understand the framework for study, you're ready to begin. One additional note: I always found it most helpful to conduct a whole class research project before releasing students to work on their independent projects. This way, children absorb the inquiry framework and begin to hone their research skills. Let's follow the four learning wheels now and see how they support and guide young researchers.

Exploring What You Already Know

Young researchers—like veterans of research—begin with their prior knowledge about their chosen topic. Ask students to brainstorm everything they already know about their question. Students can do this as a whole class experience, in small groups, or with a partner. Using either words or pictures, they might find semantic webs an effective way to represent their evolving knowledge base. Webbing works particularly well with young learners. (See example on page 100.) The brainstorming is simply a way to generate a lot of related information; there are really no right or wrong answers. Once children have listed everything they know, they may want to categorize and organize it in some way. Youngsters usually find charts quite manageable.

Habitat
adaptable
found everywhere
homes
dens

Raccoons

families
several babies

Eat
garbage
meat
vegetables
carnivores

Children may want to brainstorm on large chart paper or use my personal favorite, a learning log. Learning logs are a powerful tool for cultivating a deep understanding of a topic, rather than simply amassing lists of surface facts. Learning logs are also a helpful way to focus on and organize information. As students discover pertinent information, they can record it in their logs and retrieve it later when needed. Students can use logs to store facts and figures, list questions as they arise, record notes and hunches, and begin to synthesize and make sense of the information they are discovering. Logs are a way for children to write their way into understanding. Logs can assume many forms—a section reserved in a loose-leaf notebook, a spiral-bound notebook, or simply blank paper stapled between tagboard covers. One note of caution: Pam Bovyer Cook maintains that if students are to use learning logs effectively, they need lots of support. She suggests a three-pronged approach. The teacher

Learning logs are a powerful tool for cultivating a deep understanding of a topic, rather than simply amassing lists of surface facts.

- must do lots of modeling, showing students how to use a log and demonstrating their multiple purposes. It's best if the teacher keeps his or her own learning log and shares it regularly with students.

- should read the students' logs, check for inaccuracies, and, in general, provide students with feedback.

- should establish regular time for students to share their logs with each other.

Like everything else related to writing, there's no one right way to "do" learning logs. They are learning tools and can be used in any way that supports learning, so experiment. Here are some ideas:

Focusing. When eyes glaze over and kids look like they are losing the thread of a discussion, ask them to take a time out and focus their learning energy by jotting down their thoughts in their logs. They can then come back together and share their notes as partners or with the whole class.

Field Notes: Teacher-To-Teacher

Soon after a new school year begins, I introduce my students to learning logs. We use a separate log for each subject of the curriculum. My school purchases multiple copies of composition booklets, and I give each student four—one for literature, math, science, and social studies. I have colleagues, however, who prefer that their students use one large, combined log for all subject areas. Some find that a binder, divided into subject areas, works best. Their students write their log notes on sheets of binder paper. However you choose to organize your logs, you'll find that they allow children to participate in their own learning in a way unequaled by any other teaching device.

Rena Malkofsky
El Carmelo School
Palo Alto, California

Problem solving. Kids can pose problems and attempt to find answers. Amy, who was beginning a study of California history, posed a problem for herself in her log: If she were in charge of choosing a location to build a mission (like the ones the Spanish missionaries built in California), what building site would she choose? Amy thought about it, read several references, and found her answer.

Amy I   # 2

If you were building a mission where would you build it? And why?

I would build my mission in a vally near a lake or river or ocean. I would do this because the people would need water and I would build it in a vally because vallys are less hot and there are more animals in the vally.

Webbing. A picture is worth a thousand words. John is ready to begin researching the life of the red fox.

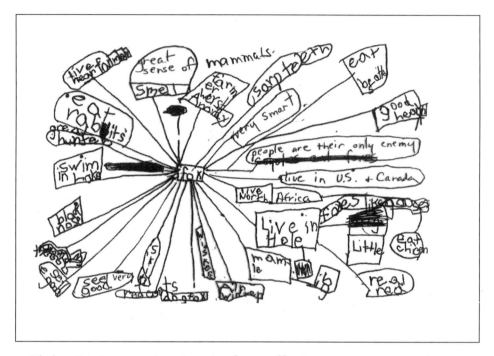

Listing. Listing questions is a simple yet effective way to get started on a research project. Here's one student's list of questions about jellyfish. Note that Joey first listed everything he knows about jellyfish before he listed what he wants to find out.

Joey

Facts I Know About Jellyfish

1. I know that jellyfish have stinging cells.

2. I know that jellyfish go to the family of Cnidaria.

Questions I have About Jellyfish

1. How do jellyfish eat?

2. What do jellyfish eat?

3. How do jellyfish move?

Responding and reacting. Kids can begin a research project by watching a video, listening to a CD, reading a picture book, or observing some physical phenomenon. Then, invite them to get out their logs and simply react. What are their first thoughts? What questions come to mind as they were experiencing the video, CD, or picture book?

Cosima, a student in Laura Schwartzberg's second-third grade P.S. 234 classroom in New York, wrote this in her learning log after observing the shrimp in the class science display.

Cosima

Observations of the shrimp
My class has 2 shrimp. The big one is Swimmy and the small one is Donnie. Swimmy is the spread of my fingers and Donnie is the size of my middle finger.

Reflecting and evaluating. At any point during their inquiry project, kids can step back and reflect on and evaluate their experience. Their questions can be as simple as "What's working for me? What's not working? What help do I need? What are my next steps?"

Schwartzberg explains her use of the double-entry journal.

> One of the most powerful tools that help children use writing to learn is the double-entry journal, developed by Anne Berthoff with her college composition students. I have adapted it for my second and third graders for work in science and social studies. It is a technique that divides each page that you write on in half, using the left side for "notes" or "observations," and the right side for "comments" or "opinions." In science, my students use double-entry journals as they study such subjects as caterpillars, snails, bones, or mystery powders. In the notes column, they record direct observations such as "They leave slime trails wherever they go." On the comments side, they record personal ideas, feelings, or opinions, such as, "The chrysalis looks like a bat hanging upside down."

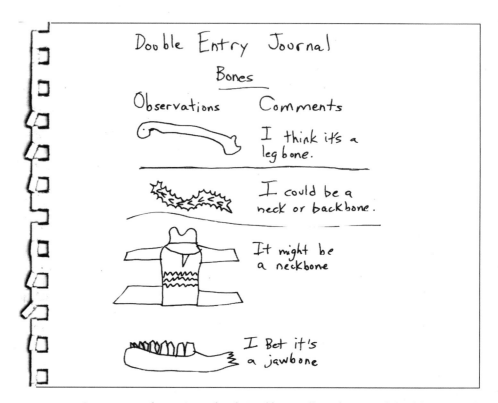

One reason that science lends itself so well to the use of double-entry journals is that as children respond to the natural world, they are given the opportunity to express their curiosity and playfulness as they learn. As they "mess around," they become scientists making important observations and learning to separate their personal feelings from observable facts. Natural or physical objects serve as the "text" that children write about.

Field Notes: Teacher-To-Teacher

Last year, the students made Observation Journals as we watched the life cycle of Painted Lady butterflies. What students choose to write in their logs helps me measure student progress in many areas. I learned a wealth of information concerning my students' levels of understanding and motivation about butterflies and their life cycle, and about their writing. I believe these students will forever remember the concepts they wrote about—much longer than labeling someone else's drawings of the life cycle on a worksheet.

Marie Therese Janise
Richard Elementary School
Acadia Parish, Louisiana

Getting Smarter through Research

Unlike fourth-grade me who relied only on an encyclopedia, your students will want to use multiple sources. Real researchers certainly spend time in the library and read everything they can get their hands on related to their topic, including newspapers, magazines, journals from historical archives, and so on; but they also talk to people who might know something about their chosen topic. Real researchers interview, conduct surveys, spend time observing the phenomenon they are researching, and, depending on the nature of the topic, may conduct a variety of experiments. There are lots of ways to find out about things, and real researchers use them all.

Field Notes: Teacher-To-Teacher

My first graders keep a running wall chart of *Ways We Learn*. Periodically, we pause to reflect on what we have learned and how, adding new kinds of sources to our chart. Because we date the entries on our chart, we have a record of increasing sophistication as researchers. For example, a September entry, based on a class study, might read "Ask a farmer" in reference to our study of cotton, while April entries, based on individual research, might read "Make a chart of how far toads can hop" or "Survey the class to find out who is afraid of snakes."

Sherry Swain
Overstreet Elementary School
Starkville, Mississippi

Students can pick up all sorts of valuable information by studying illustrations.

Nonfiction resources. In recent years, nonfiction materials for children have proliferated. There now exists a quantity of very readable nonfiction literature that addresses an array of physical, social, and biological phenomena. Also consider bringing in adult reference materials. Even if children are unable to read the adult books, the photographs, illustrations, maps, and diagrams the books may contain can be a rich and visually accessible source of information. Students can pick up all sorts of valuable information by studying illustrations. You can also read aloud from these books, helping students record the information in their own words.

Fiction. Well-written children's fiction often contains factual information. Through the aesthetics of story, fiction can transport children into new realms of knowing. For example, as children read Patricia MacLachlan's *Sarah Plain and Tall,* they can feel and see the blue vastness of the

SHOPTALK

Freeman, Evelyn B. and Diane Goetz Person, eds. *Using Nonfiction Trade Books in the Elementary Classroom: From Ants to Zeppelins.* Urbana, Illinois: National Council of Teachers of English, 1992.

New York City teacher Laura Schwartzberg recommends these resources for identifying helpful children's fiction and nonfiction. She writes, "*Using Nonfiction Trade Books in the Elementary Classroom* is a wonderful sourcebook for teachers who want to learn more about the genre of nonfiction. Many contributors, classroom teachers, librarians, college professors, and children's authors examine the link between nonfiction and the elementary curriculum. There is a wealth of information ranging from descriptions of specific books on a particular topic to full thematic units. The collection contains numerous suggestions for classroom activities and features an extensive bibliography."

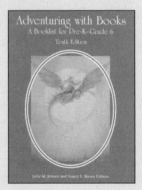

National Council of Teachers of English. *Adventuring with Books: A Booklist for Pre-K–Grade 6.* Urbana, Illinois: NCTE, 1992.

This is another wonderful collection of annotated booklists on subjects including fantasy, historical fiction, science, biography, and many more. The descriptions of books are succinct and clear.

American Library Association. *Book Links.* Chicago, Illinois: ALA.

Each issue of this bimonthly magazine helps teachers integrate books into the classroom with articles that revolve around themes in literature, social studies, science, and other areas. I've found suggestions for author studies and articles on themes such as Ancient Egypt, Growing Things, and the Seashore. There are extensive bibliographies and suggestions for book discussions and classroom activities.

prairie sky as they learn about the small details that governed the daily lives of prairie settlers more than a century ago. Taro Yashima's *Umbrella* gives children a gentle sense of the American-Japanese urban experience, through an interweaving of Japanese characters and words with illustrations of New York City streets. Do include fiction—novels, short stories, picture books—on your resource table.

Community funds of knowledge. While we assign textbook chapters to our students to read, a whole world outside calls to us. Let's listen! Following the lead of the inspiring Foxfire Project (1987), we'll want to encourage our students to enter the community and visit relevant places and people. We'll also want to open the doors of our classrooms and invite visitors in from the community. We want our students to understand that sometimes the best source of information is another human being.

Luis Moll of the University of Arizona has devoted much of his research (1992) to exploring the ways in which schools can embrace and learn from their surrounding communities. He talks about the "funds of knowledge" that every community possesses. Around the corner from the school, you'll find Dick Friedlander, a contractor who has built homes in the area for thirty years. He can tell you everything there is to know about carpentry, plumbing, electrical work, and so forth. Want to know more about dogs? Talk to Rose and George Dagavarian who own the grooming shop, Paws R Us. They love dogs and raise championship collies. They also love kids and would welcome the opportunity to talk with your class. And don't forget Bob's Donuts. Bob Holt has been rising at 3 am every morning for twenty years. Let him talk with the kids about creating and managing a small business (besides, he brings free samples!). You get the idea. By tapping the funds of knowledge in your community, you can bring a wealth of information into your classroom.

We want our students to understand that sometimes the best source of information is another human being.

Depending on their ages, students can take a leading role in contacting local experts and visitors and making the necessary arrangements. With practice, students can also learn how to create a thoughtful interview that will yield lots of richly detailed information. And don't forget to tap the funds of knowledge right inside your own classroom or school. Parents, teachers, and the students themselves can be sources of all sorts of fascinating information. (Remember Roberto, my rabbit expert?)

My son, Brennan, attends Ohlone Elementary School in Palo Alto, California. At the start of every school year, Ohlone parents receive a questionnaire asking them to list their professions, interests, hobbies, and talents. These are kept in a file in the school office. As Ohlone teachers begin a new unit of study, they can check this funds of knowledge file and call parents who might know something about the chosen topic. Brennan's dad is a geologist. Every year, he is asked to talk with Ohlone students about scaling the cliffs of East Greenland, drilling deep into the earth for rock samples, and analyzing veins in rocks for minerals. There's simply no learning substitute for a riveting firsthand account of someone who's been there and done that!

Several years ago, Toby Curry, a teacher at the Dewey Center for Urban Education, helped facilitate a project for kids ages ten through twelve during the summer months. Curry explains, "We interviewed community residents and toured parts of the city. The funds of knowledge we discovered in our Detroit neighborhood were unknown heroes and heroines who chose to live and work in our struggling inner-city community."

Media: films, videos, laserdiscs, and the Internet. Pam Adair teaches third grade at Fair Oaks School. Most of her children speak Spanish; some have never attended school before and are not yet literate in either Spanish or English. Nonetheless, Adair engaged them in a sophisticated study of Martin Luther King, Jr., and the American Civil Rights movement. How did she do it?

Exploring her local library, she found copies of *Life* magazines dating from the early sixties with striking black and white photographs the Civil Rights marches, cafeteria sit-down strikes, and the Atlanta bus boycott. Her students spent hours leafing through the magazines and drinking in the dramatic images. At the same time, Adair brought in audiotapes of songs from the Civil Rights movement; the children listened to Mahalia Jackson singing "We Shall Overcome," and T-Bone Johnson wailing mournful blues songs on his harmonica. She also collected old newsreels on video.

SHOPTALK

Claggett, Fran with Joan Brown.
*Drawing Your Own Conclusions:
Graphic Strategies for Reading, Writing,
and Thinking.* Portsmouth, New
Hampshire: Heinemann, 1992.

Oakland, California, teacher Pam Bovyer
Cook gives *Drawing Your Own Conclusions* her highest recommendation. "This book is written by two high school English teachers.
The ideas are applicable to all ages. It shows how graphics allow all
students, especially special needs students such as second language
learners, gifted, unmotivated, and learning disabled, make meaning
as they read and write. The book is full of student samples and has
lots of strategies and applications. When students draw in response
to what they've read, discussed, or written, they are making visual-
ized connections to their own lives. The authors show how graphics
are a rich way of learning and understanding and make for exciting
and accessible involvement for all students."

The children watched, analyzed, and discussed the grainy black-and-white
images they saw reflected on the video screen. Adair used written materials
by reading aloud to her students: newspaper clippings, children's literature,
the speeches of Martin Luther King, Jr., and the poetry of Langston Hughes
and Gwendolyn Brooks.

In this way, even though her students were limited in their ability to access
information through written references, they were able to engage in a fairly
sophisticated study of a complex period of American history. The end result
was a book of illustrations and captions they composed highlighting what
they had learned about the Civil Rights movement (Bridges 1995).

If your school is wired to the Internet, then you have access to a world of information. Pam Bovyer Cook, who teaches fifth-sixth grade, writes, "Last
year we were reading Scott O'Dell's *Black Star Bright Dawn* about the
Iditerod, the sled dog race across Alaska's frozen tundra. We found a school
in Alaska and also an Internet address where we could track the race and
keep abreast of developments as the race progressed. It brought the race home
to us and was a fabulous learning experience in all ways."

Artifacts. What could be more exciting than viewing, touching, listening to,
smelling, and perhaps even tasting a real specimen or object? (Provided you're

not studying banana slugs!) As much as possible, we should find ways to bring in materials that our students can actually hold and experience. If you have access to a museum, check with the director to see whether it offers lending kits. Students may also bring in artifacts from home. For example, when students in Rena Malkofsky's fifth grade at El Carmelo School in Palo Alto, California, studied architecture and building, they examined architectural models, blueprints, and designs before becoming involved in their own building experience. How would they design and build a coat rack that would fit in a corner of their classroom and yet accommodate all thirty students' coats, sweaters, and hats? Handling and experiencing the real stuff of architectural design brought the learning to life.

In sum, real researchers use multiple sources as they investigate their subjects. Rarely do they consult an encyclopedia, a secondary source of information. Yet, generations of children have grown up believing that copying an encyclopedia for a school report constitutes research. As students participate in a variety of research projects, they discover a wide range of available sources of information. They will also begin to realize that there are no easy answers. The world is infinitely complex and subtle. Indeed, students are likely to encounter multiple opinions. One of the jobs of a real researcher is to sort out fact from fiction, reliable information from unreliable.

As students explore all these resources, they will need to keep track of their information as they discover it. There are no hard and fast rules about where to store information. Learning logs work well as do index cards stored in a small recipe or file box. While there are no rules for how to collect and store the information, there is one big rule for how to record it: students must write in their own words.

While there are no rules for how to collect and store the information, there is one big rule for how to record it: students must write in their own words.

Whales can float in water because its blubber is lighter than water and because its air is lighter than water and they are endangered species and when a whale is diving it goes up three times and then it goes down to the bottom of the water and a father whale is named a bull and a mother whale is named a cow and a baby whale is named a calf.

SHOPTALK

Atwell, Nancie, ed. *Coming to Know: Writing to Learn in the Intermediate Grades.* Portsmouth, New Hampshire: Heinemann, 1990.

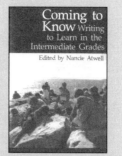

Fourteen classroom teachers detail the strategies and materials they use to support their students' research across the curriculum. The book includes four valuable appendices: a list of different genres kids can use to publish their research, guiding questions for learning logs, lists of thematically related fiction and nonfiction books, and professional and commercial resources for both teachers and students that support reading and writing to learn.

Simply telling students, "You must write in your own words," however, won't make it happen. Conducting research is something of an art, requiring specific know-how and skills. I didn't learn how to do research until I was in college. As we most certainly don't want our students to wait until they are college-bound to discover the satisfaction of conducting original research and finding answers to questions that matter to them, we need to carefully consider the skills that are required to do research and teach them. Indeed, in order to make sure our students are prepared to engage in research, we should take time each day to demonstrate a specific research technique.

What Researchers Need To Know

My guide to helping my students become researchers is Donald Graves' *Investigate Nonfiction* (1990). I've tried Graves' ideas with my own students, found they worked well, so I'll share them with you. You might also consider buying his book.

Skimming. Our students need to learn that when they are reading quantities of material, they don't need to read everything in detail, nor should they. We need to help them learn how quickly to take in headers, key phrases, diagrams, charts, photo captions, and the like, so that they can get a global sense of the material. Then, they can quickly ascertain which material they can abandon and which material they should set aside for further, more detailed reading.

My daughter returned home from her sixth-grade class the other afternoon with the assignment to ask her mom or dad to skim a social studies textbook chapter with her. Although I'll admit I wasn't thrilled to have to skim the chapter (I had hoped never again in my lifetime to have to read another social studies textbook!), I appreciated the assignment. Her teacher knows

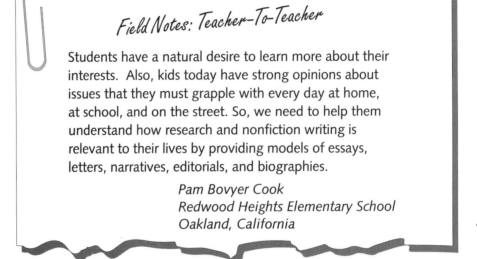

Field Notes: Teacher-To-Teacher

Students have a natural desire to learn more about their interests. Also, kids today have strong opinions about issues that they must grapple with every day at home, at school, and on the street. So, we need to help them understand how research and nonfiction writing is relevant to their lives by providing models of essays, letters, narratives, editorials, and biographies.

Pam Bovyer Cook
Redwood Heights Elementary School
Oakland, California

that skimming is tricky business, requiring lots of help and multiple demonstrations from an older, more experienced reader.

Note-Taking. Learning to take notes selectively and concisely is a skill that also requires demonstration and discussion. Initially, children are inclined to copy verbatim everything they read. Working on an overhead transparency, we can show children how a skilled note-taker operates: reading everything quickly, then jotting down in his or her own words brief phrases, not complete sentences, which capture the essence of the message. Graves suggests the following instructional sequence:

1. Students skim the material.
2. Then they close the book and tell a partner what they read.
3. Keeping the book closed, students jot down in their own words what they read.
4. Students share their notes with a partner and explain how and why they recorded what they did.

Interviewing. I'm a self-confessed National Public Radio junkie. One of my favorite shows is "Fresh Air" with Terry Gross. Gross is a skilled interviewer, knowing how to ask questions tactfully that nudge her guests past the routine answers. Listening to Gross has convinced me that conducting an effective interview is an art. Learning how to ask the right questions requires careful thought and planning. You can help your students develop effective interviewing techniques by providing numerous in-classroom demonstrations.

Explain that you'd like to interview a student to demonstrate how interviews are conducted and ask for volunteers. Once you've selected your volunteer, interview him or her about an object or issue you know he or she knows a lot about. Then invite your students to analyze and critique the interview, listing and examining the sorts of questions you asked.

Next, students can work as partners interviewing each other about a particular subject. Again, a reflective post-interview session can help students identify which questions work well and why, and which questions seem to dead-end. In turn, your students can develop criteria for effective interviews.

Observing. Observing, record-keeping, and categorizing are important research skills, particularly for the scientist. Inviting students to keep logs observing some physical phenomena is an effective way to develop these skills.

Melissa, age six, is a passionate observer of the two pet mice housed in Arlene Malkin's first-second grade classroom at Ohlone Elementary School. She notes in her journal the small details of their daily lives: how much they eat and drink, the times of day they run in their exercise wheel, how long they sleep. So intently does Melissa stare at these mice that her teacher confessed to me she thinks Melissa has developed x-ray eyes. How would you explain this illustration that Malkin found in Melissa's learning log?!

a mose sklatih

Comparing, categorizing, classifying. As students are gathering information from many sources, they must find ways to organize it so that it makes sense to them. A simple beginning is to think in terms of similarities and differences: How might things be related or not? Marty Morgenbesser, who teaches second grade in Santa Rosa, California, remembers his student, Sam, who decided to conduct an experiment on "things that break and things that don't."

Our students will have acquired a critical problem-solving tool once they understand that quantities of information can be classified according to any number of attributes. Grappling with real data that they have collected themselves can naturally lead students to grouping systems that help them structure and analyze their findings.

How soon can you begin to teach report-writing skills such as identifying resources, collecting data, and note-taking? Beth Huntzinger, first-grade teacher at the Columbia School in Sunnyvale, California, finds that even her first graders are capable of simple data-gathering procedures. "They love to write attribute books that tell, in simple language 'all about' a topic. For example, one of my seven-year-old students wrote a report entitled, 'All About Chimpanzees,' listing everything he knew about chimps."

chimps

Illustrated BY
BY Ryan Pieper Ryan Pieper

chimpanzeos Life in
africa and they have
enumees. they are
Meen. and Frsum.
They are good with
hands and climbing.
they are cute.

1

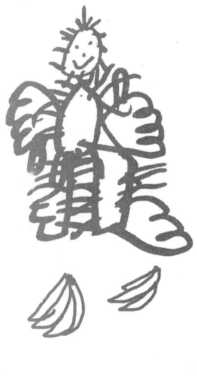

More hair on thir body
then People One of
thir calls is loud hooting.
They have Black hair
chimps have no tails.
you Do not Undrstad them.

2

they're very Smart.
chimps are as Smart
as my Sister Angie
She's 4.
They are mammal

3

no hair on face
& hands. Boy
chimps are 5 ft.
tall + ways 120 Pounds.
They eat Froot and
nuts they live in the
Forest in Africa

4

The age of three
they can Yues the
tools to Kech termites
I hrd on the News
chimps wer in
Dangrd Spee shees.

5

Becoming an Expert

We bring the process of learning to a complete circle when we have the opportunity to share with others what we have learned. In other words, we shape, refine, and extend our learning as we explain to others the meaning and significance of our learning experiences. Simply stated, the best way to learn is to teach. Ironically, this critical presenting step has often been left out of traditional schooling practices. If children share at all, it seldom extends beyond a written report which is turned into an audience of one—the teacher—who is often largely concerned with red-circling mistakes.

In striking contrast, teachers who invite their students to participate in research projects make sure they also provide them with the time and resources needed to share with a real audience that may even extend beyond the classroom door.

At Sunnyslope School in Phoenix, Arizona, for example, a master list of resident student experts is posted in the school auditorium. Classrooms may contact the expert and request a presentation. As the requests come in, student experts travel from classroom to classroom with their research portfolios—which may contain maps, flow charts, slides, and physical specimens—sharing with their schoolmates the findings of their research.

We bring the process of learning to a complete circle when we have the opportunity to share with others what we have learned.

As children conduct their research, they should feel free to use a variety of media—sketches, diagrams, charts and so forth—to capture and organize their information. And certainly, when they present their research, they should have a wide variety of presentational formats from which to choose. As your students will discover, it's quite a feat knowing how to transfer information from one format to another as you learn to represent your learning to yourself and to others.

So, too, is the process you need to engage in as you determine which format is appropriate for your data and findings. Not all formats are equally appropriate for all data. Students will need to carefully consider the nature of their data and design a format that will best showcase it. Below are suggestions for ways in which students can share their research. Give it to them and let them choose. It can be adapted to various grade levels.

Letters to the editor. If you have some new information or have developed a unique perspective on a particular issue that you would like to share with the public, consider writing to the editor of your local newspaper or to the editor of an appropriate magazine or journal. Explain what you did, what you found, and why you have assumed your particular stance.

SHOPTALK

Gamberg, Ruth, Winnifred Kwak, Meredith Hutchings and Judy Altheim with Gail Edwards. *Learning and Loving It: Theme Studies in the Classroom.* Portsmouth, New Hampshire: Heinemann, 1988.

After constructing a 7 x 5 foot playhouse on the playground, a class of six-, seven-, and eight-year-olds at the award-winning Dalhousie School in Nova Scotia turned enthusiastically to a theme cycle on "Houses of the World." They brainstormed research questions, researched using a variety of reference materials, and categorized and charted the information. After weeks of study, they constructed accurately detailed models. As a culmination of the study, the students held a learning fair and invited parents and friends. The young researchers displayed their models along with descriptive books and posters. They stood by their displays, explaining what they had learned to the interested visitors. This theme cycle is one of six which are described in inspiring detail. It will help you understand the critical difference between a traditional thematic unit with "paste-on" activities and a core of the curriculum theme cycle. From the latter flows multiple opportunities for authentic reading, writing, researching, and presenting. This is a book I wouldn't want to be without.

Poster sessions, bulletin board. Create a poster or bulletin board display with headlines and captions, charts, diagrams, and so on, and explain it to the class. Be prepared to answer questions.

Scrapbook or photo album. Arrange your notes, pictures, graphs, or articles in a scrapbook or photo album and write a description of your research process and findings.

Oral histories and interviews. Transcribe tapes from your interviews and present with photographs, artwork, artifacts, and background information.

Newspaper. Create an edition that is related to a historical time period. Every article, editorial, advertisement, and so on should reflect the time period you studied.

Surveys, interviews, questionnaires. Design tools for collecting additional information.

Slide or video presentation. Represent your findings through a video or slide presentation. Write an accompanying script. Pam Bovyer Cook recommends the software *Kid Pix Companions*, available from Broderbund, to help create computerized slide shows.

Big Books. Present research through Big Books that you can design and bind yourself. In her New York City School, P.S. 234, second-third grade teacher Laura Schwartzberg's students created Big Books about various topics they studied, including the human body, houses, and airports.

Tableaux. Oakland, California, teacher Pam Bovyer Cook says that tableaux are a fun and successful way to share learning. What are tableaux and how do they work? Bovyer Cook explains. "A group of students make 'frozen pictures' with their bodies while a narrator reads a text. Each group may present six to eight tableaux. The audience closes their eyes between the scenes. The teacher or another student can shake a tambourine to facilitate the transition between scenes."

Debate or panel discussion. Present and debate your positions on an issue if you worked with a partner or as part of a group, and you reached different conclusions. Or present your findings as a panel; be prepared to field questions from the audience. One member should serve as the moderator.

Models and maps. Create cross-sections, dioramas, shadow boxes, mobiles, relief maps—life-size or to scale.

Diagrams, tables, graphs, flowcharts, timelines. Chart the sequential steps involved in making something. If you conducted an experiment, diagram the steps you followed. Represent the chronology of a historical event you studied. You can also capture this information in a how-to book, written so someone else can follow your procedure.

Role-playing, sociodrama. Role-play to present a biography. Try sociodrama for a dramatic presentation of a historical or current sociopolitical event.

Folk art, songs, dances, food. Present and describe folk art from the time period or region you studied. Perform representational songs and dances. Give us a taste of your project by preparing regional or ethnic food. Prepare enough for everyone to sample and include recipes.

Museum kits. Create an attractive display of objects that represents your topic and provide written explanations.

What about Evaluation?

As students pursue their independent research, you'll want to conduct frequent conferences with them to determine what is working, what isn't, what their goals are, and how they're working to achieve their goals. Evaluation, in other words, is not something that happens just at the end of the research project, but is continuous as teachers, students, and (if possible) parents work together on the evolving project.

Discuss with your students the characteristics of effective research. Talk about the criteria you'll use to evaluate both the process and completion of each research project. We want our students to understand what constitutes effective research and to work hard to meet that criteria in their own research projects. Pat Collins (1990), a sixth-grade teacher in Northhampton, Massachusetts, developed the following criteria to evaluate her students' research. She assigned each category a ten-point value:

1. Research questions were carefully thought out
2. Used class time well
3. Took careful notes
4. Showed a willingness to revise and improve drafts
5. Edited the piece carefully before submitting it to me for editing
6. Submitted all work to me with the final draft
7. Showed creativity and careful thought
8. Correctly completed bibliography
9. Completed work on time
10. Project presentation format enhanced the research

Our students have lifetimes of experiences, the starting point for new learning.

Making Connections to Lifelong Learning

Beginning with what we know, we make connections to what we are coming to know. Our students have lifetimes of experiences, the starting point for new learning. Students always begin a research project by identifying what they already know about the chosen topic of study and building from there. As reflective learners, they connect what they've learned to their own lives and to important issues of contemporary society. And they reveal their understanding to the extent that they can use their new knowledge and skills in novel ways.

One line of inquiry leads to another; this is, perhaps, the hallmark of real research. The measure of true learning is not recall of old material, but new questions that address new possibilities, leading the learner into new realms of exploration. So research projects end not with the question, "What did you learn?" but "What will you learn next?"

Chapter 7

Journals, Poetry, and Other Reasons To Write

Like my daughter, I kept a journal when I was ten, eleven, and twelve. I called mine a diary and hid it in the valance above my bedroom window. My diaries came from Woolworth's. They were covered with blue, pink, or white vinyl. Golden curlicues danced around the gold-edged pages, and each book sported a lock that anyone could jimmy open with a safety pin or paper clip. So much for securing secret thoughts!

These days we invite our students to write in a journal. Some teachers require that their students write daily in one. I've visited many classrooms where children dutifully pull out their journals and record a daily thought ("I went to the park") with about as much soul and feeling as they might muster for a worksheet. This isn't writing.

Journals can be an easy way to invite children into the writing world, but children won't want to stay and play if the journal writing becomes a laborious requirement with little meaning. How can we make journal writing meaningful?

Write Back

Several teachers—including Nancie Atwell (1987) and Sara Mosle (1995)—describe letter writing in journals, also known as interactive dialogue journals. They invite their children to write to them and they write back, asking

First of all, the dialogue journal is truly an opportunity to get to know your students.

Field Notes: Teacher-To-Teacher

Dixie, a teacher in an ongoing staff development group I was leading, came to a September meeting reporting that her second grade students had been dutifully writing in their journals but that they weren't excited about the journals and that they seldom chose to journal when given other choices. Through our discussion, Dixie came to realize that those of us who used journals most successfully incorporated a journal-sharing time into each day. This is a time when volunteers can read from their journals, a time for children to learn from each other's writing, a time for the teacher to spotlight breakthroughs and evidence of growth. Dixie returned to her classroom, initiated a journal sharing time and became a spokesperson for the power of sharing journals as a way to promote fluency. At each of the remaining sessions, Dixie shared student growth based on journals, and each time she reminded us that the invitation to share with an audience is a magic motivation for journal writing.

Sherry Swain
Overstreet Elementary School
Starkville, Mississippi

questions, commenting on shared anecdotes—carving out time to enjoy a personal written conversation with each child. I know it's time-consuming to keep interactive journals. I've always kept them with my graduate students and have spent hours each week responding to as many as fifty journals. Nevertheless, the benefits for me as a teacher were always worth the effort.

Third-grade teacher Marie Therese Janise uses dialogue journals to exchange weekly thoughts on reading material. The students write to her about what they are reading, and she writes back. She asks them questions about the reading, sharing her own thoughts and in all ways encouraging their active, thoughtful reading and writing.

First of all, the dialogue journal is truly an opportunity to get to know your students. In the rush of classroom activity, it's almost impossible to find the quiet time necessary to enjoy a meaningful conversation with each individual student. Their personal thoughts and private lives often remain unknown

Dear, Mrs. Janise,

I've been reading A book called WHEN DINOSAURS RULED THE EARTH. It is a good book. My faviot Dinosaur was Brachiosaurus BRAK-ee-uh-SOR-us. Do you have a favot Din.

Sin ed
Matt

Dear Matthew,

I was wondering why Brachiosaurus is your favorite dinosaur.
I think Triceratops is my favorite because all of the adults would gather around the young to protect them from harm. Elephants do the same thing.

Your teacher,
Mrs. Janise

to us unless we find time to talk to each one about the small details of their daily lives that extend beyond the classroom door. And knowing our students is essential to helping them. When we understand our students as unique individuals, then we're in a more effective position to help them; to respond in ways that might make a difference for them both personally and academically.

It's a reciprocal process. As we respond to our students' lives, we tend to share incidents from our own lives. Before long, we've established a real relationship. We cease to be that mysterious teacher who our students think eats and sleeps and lives at school. We become real people with real questions and interests and lives. Sharing written conversations through journals enables our students to know and care about us as real human beings. And it's caring, compassionate relationships that build our classroom communities.

Sharing written conversations through journals enables our students to know and care about us as real human beings

Sara Mosle teaches more than thirty third graders in Washington Heights, a predominantly Dominican and African American community that extends some forty-five blocks from Harlem to the northern tip of Manhattan. In this overcrowded neighborhood, drugs are rife and people struggle with the many complications of poverty.

In a demanding classroom situation that simply didn't allow time for friendly chats, Mosle (1995) found that journals enabled her to converse with each child. They become her lifeline to each child. Mosle says, "The journals operated a little like an apartment-house air shaft, providing a common area where we could communicate. Like neighbors leaning out of the windows, we exchanged gossip, inquired after family, caught glimpses of one

SHOPTALK

Whiteley, Opal. *Opal: The Journal of an Understanding Heart.* New York: Crown Trade Books, 1984.

Here's a book you should read. It may help you as a teacher, but most importantly, it will touch you as a human being. Opal was a six-year-old orphan living in the rough and tumble world of the turn-of-the-century Oregon lumber camps when she penned her vivid, poetic observations of nature, human relationships, and her emerging understanding of life. Sensitive, compassionate, and heart-breakingly innocent, Opal is both a remarkable writer and a human being. I love this book. So do my three children.

another's lives. They wrote freely, I think, partly because they were also writing to themselves." They wrote to seek advice, to describe events in their lives, to take Mosle to task for perceived injustices like an unpopular seating arrangement, and to share their hopes and fears and dreams. In the process, Mosle discovered themes that reverberated in her own life. The journals helped her understand her students' lives in relation to her own, enabling her to bridge the gap between home and school.

Susan Raedeke who teaches third grade in Crown Point, Indiana, opens up the interactive journals she shares with students to family members as well. She refers to these journals as "connection notebooks," and she invites parents and family members to participate in an ongoing written conversation with herself and their child. Writing in the notebook is strictly invitational. Parents need not participate; but over the course of the school year, Raedeke finds that nearly every family chooses to write at least once. As Raedeke explains, the notebook is meant "to connect learning that occurs in school with learning at home." The notebook enables teacher and parents to become "partners" in their child's education. Here's an entry from Carly's journal. She begins by posing the question, "Do you remember when you were nine?" Her mother responds with her nine-year-old memory. Then her brother, Cyril, adds his own memory. Raedeke responds.

> Tonight I will read "When I was Nine." Do you remember when you were nine?
>
> On Palm Sunday, 1958 when I was nine years old, I was baptized by immersion. There were about six or seven other kids baptized at the same time. We had finished a 3 month bible course, passed a written test, and made public confessions of faith before we could do this. Next to this, my wedding day, and the births of my children this was the most important day of my entire life!   —Mom
>
> When I was nine I had the best teacher in the world. She was Mrs. Raedeke.
>   Cyril.
>
> Thank you Cyril. I remember having a special boy in my class that year. He was good at making cranes.

Toby Curry, who teaches sixth grade, is also an enthusiastic advocate of a parent-teacher journal. Curry explains.

> My favorite journal is a "roving parent journal." One student, Margarita, keeps a calendar of who gets to take the journal home each day. I've learned to send home a photocopy of my response to the previous parent and send the journal on the next day with another student. The journal is a great model of adult literacy for the kids and a wonderful place for the parents and me to discuss curriculum and parenting skills.

Field Notes: Teacher-To-Teacher

Written conversations can be useful for beginning writers and reluctant writers—particularly those who are afraid to take risks both with spelling and the creation of a message. My student Shelly used to refuse to write without her bottle of white-out. Writing back and forth with me finally freed her from the fear of making a mistake. Written conversations, in their simplest form, involve two writers, usually a teacher and student, who converse on paper. This provides an informal and supportive context for writing where the focus is on the message, not the surface features of the writing. Also, the audience is available to provide feedback immediately!

Margie Leys
Waga Waga, New South Wales

Just like all aspects of your writing program, you'll want to experiment with journals and find the way that works best for you and your students. You might try letting children exchange journals and write to each other. Or, perhaps, children don't need to write in them every day, but only when they have thoughts and ideas that call for a written outlet.

First-grade teacher Sherry Swain reminds us that young children may need to draw in journals before they write. Swain explains.

> First grader Will came to me as an artist, filling page after page in his journal with detailed drawings of helicopters and trains in action. After several weeks of applauding his drawings and the accompanying stories he told as he shared his pictures, I began to think about how to nudge him to include text along with his drawings. Then one day as I was reading artist Walter Anderson's *Horn Island Logs* in which Anderson

recorded his thoughts and feelings about the wildlife he painted, I wrote
an entry in my own journal about the richness the log entries brought
to the art. I read my journal aloud that day, and smiled at Will as I finished. Thereafter Will began to add text in explanation of his drawings,
"Just like that other artist," he winked.

As your students explore and experiment with journals, they may come to
share Juliann Lin's passion for journals. Juliann, a fifth grader in Montreal,
Quebec, clearly finds her journal invaluable.

Why I Like Journals
by Julianna Lin

My favourite lesson is journal because I like to write things. When I'm doing journal, I can write down anything on any topic. One day I can write the beginning of a story. Since I'm not obliged to finish the story, the next day I can write a poem. When I'm writing a journal, I'm free to explore "The Forest of Topics." There after picking a tree, or topic, I explore my topic further. If I happen to have crossed "The Field of Imagination," I'd write an imaginative story (or poem). I'd search around my tree (topic) to find some imaginative thing to write.

If I happen to have splashed through "The River of Humour," I'd write a funny story (or poem) or a story (or poem) with many jokes in it. If I happen to have taken a swim in "The River of Knowledge," I'd write a story (or poem) with true facts in it. If I happen to wade across "The River Twist," I'd write a story (or poem) with a twist at the end.

However, before exploring this "forest" I must decide whether to write a story or a poem. That is all one needs to know before entering the forest.

When I'm writing my journal, I can explore this forest that extends farther than the eye can see, even more. That is why I like journal.

What about Other Genres?

Writing allows us access to the world. It's a marvelous tool that enables us to perform many functions. But writing has form as well as function and we want our students to understand these various forms or genres and to be able to use them correctly. How do you teach students to write a persuasive essay? a parody? an observational report? In general, when introducing children to a new genre, it's helpful to think in terms of a four-step process.

1. First, immerse your students in the genre you want them to learn. Provide them with many potent examples. Read the examples out loud—two, three, four or more times. Post examples around the room, and invite your students to find their own examples and bring them in to share.

2. Talk about the genre. Help children understand the unique qualities of the persuasive essay or the business letter or any genre you want them to become familiar with.

3. Demonstrate your own writing in the chosen genre. Talk out loud as you grapple with refining your example, emphasizing the unique qualities that distinguish it from other genres.

4. Finally, after children have heard the genre read aloud, read it for themselves, discussed it, and watched you play with it, let them try their hand at it—and invite them to share their writing.

Let's see how this process might work with poetry. In Rena Malkofsky's fifth-grade class, students were assigned different poems to memorize each week, then the kids decided that they each wanted to choose their own. Carly and Julie became hooked on Langston Hughes. Each week they chose a different poem by Hughes to recite, and introduced the poem in different voices pretending they were various relatives or friends of his. One week they were his granddaughters, the next they were his neighbors. The class came to expect and look forward to their next Langston Hughes experience.

Julie
Carly

Julie : Were gonna recite a little old poem by our grand pappy Langston Hughs, C'man sister tell these youngsters the name.

Carly : The name. . . . The name. . . . uh . . . oh I just can't do it.

Julie: Go on girl you can do it!

Carly: O.K. The name . . . of this poem is
Old Walt

together   Old Walt by Langston Hughs
(Cindy, Julie)

Old man walt Went finding
and seeking

finding less than sought seeker
more than found
every detail minder of the seeker
and finding

Anything from your own life experiences can become a poem.

Sharing Poetry with Children

Poetry should be an everyday event. If we want children to really know and love poetry, we must surround them with the voices of many poets—every day. Be on the lookout for those poetic moments in which you can slip in a poem—while waiting for the lunch bell, on a bus headed for a field trip, as a greeting to begin a new school day. Poetry blooms from the ordinary, from the small details of daily living. As children become familiar with the voice of poetry, they learn to write their own poetry.

Poet Georgia Heard reminds us that "poetry begins with something you care about." Children will find their way into poetry when you invite them to think about things that matter to them. Sharing your own poetry writing is a powerful way to lure children into poetry.

Think out loud as you lead children along the path *you* follow as you create a poem. Here's one possible pathway. You'll want to experiment, however, and find a way that works best for you.

Think about something that you really care about—something deep from within the warmth of your own life material. It could be the memory of a favorite teacher, your trips to the ocean as a child, or a steaming bowl of oatmeal. Anything from your own life experiences can become a poem.

Once you have a topic or theme for your poem, you might begin by simply listing out everything that comes to you about your chosen topic. List poems provide an easy entry into poetry (Graves 1994). Working on a blackboard, chart paper, or an overhead projector, quickly generate a list in front of the children. Without hesitating, capture words, images, sounds, smells, whatever dances into your mind. Try working with nouns—listing out the specific things that surround your poetic memory.

When you have your list, step back and reflect (again, out loud, so the children can follow your composing process). Explain that the free association or brainstorming that you just did is very similar to the sketching a visual artist does. In your quick sketching of words, you are capturing your feelings. The words reflect your overall impression of the topic of your poem. Ask the children what they see in your words. "What was I thinking about when I was sketching with words?"

Now invite children to create their own list poems. You can do this first as a whole class; invite the children to generate a class list poem. Once you feel sure they understand the process, they can return to their seats and create their own list poems around their own personal memories, incidents, discoveries, and passions.

You'll want to respond to the children's poetry in the same way you respond to all their writing. First, to accept the poem with care and, then, to listen hard as children read out loud. Once the children have finished reading, share with them what you heard.

There are many ways to introduce children to poetry. Donald Graves (1994) doesn't like to give children poetry line starters, but he says that he has found two lines, in particular, helpful:

- I am the person who...

- Remember me...

S H O P T A L K

Heard, Georgia. *For the Good of the Earth and Sun: Teaching Poetry.* Portsmouth, New Hampshire: Heinemann, 1989.

For those of you who feel uncomfortable around poetry, this book will help. Written for teachers of all grade levels, it's a book about teaching poetry, but it doesn't provide a formula to elicit poetry from students. Rather, it offers a method of teaching poetry that respects the intelligence and originality of both teacher and student. Step by step, you'll become more familiar with the world of poetry and will learn not to feel uncomfortable or afraid of it.

SHOPTALK

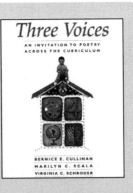

Cullinan, Bernice E., Marilyn C. Scala and Virginia C. Schroder. *Three Voices: An Invitation to Poetry across the Curriculum.* York, Maine: Stenhouse Publishers, 1995.

If ever you doubted poetry's place in a well-rounded curriculum, this book will convince you that poetry is truly not just an add-on or an enrichment activity. The key is to know where to start and how to develop teaching ideas that make poetry a natural and enjoyable part of classroom work. *Three Voices* is organized around strategies for using poetry. Thirty-three detailed strategies are spelled out and nearly three hundred brief idea suggestions are packed into this gem of a book. In addition, sidebars contain information on such topics as criteria and a checklist for selecting the kinds of poetry children like, as well as descriptions of poetry forms. After you read this book, you'll add your voice to the authors, singing the praises of poetry in the classroom.

Toby Curry shares another way to invite children into poetry.

A wonderful Michigan poet, Laurence Pike, got incredible responses from kids at our school by inviting them to write "I am" poems. My favorite was written by a young boy named Jason, whom I hardly knew. Jason had just come to our school from out of state. After I told Jason how incredible his poem was, he said, "Gee, I didn't know I was a writer until I met you, Mrs. Curry."

I Am

by Jason

I am an energetic cougar
trying to be the best.
I am a sensational saxophone memorizing
the glamorous tunes of Kenny G.
I am a spicy rib so hot
that ice water can't cool me down.
I am a lost planet wandering out in space
waiting for someone to confirm me.
I am Jason W. a little species, running around on earth
that only mother nature knows about.

Virginia Schroeder (Cullinan 1995) who teaches at Munsey Park School in Manhasset, New York, offers an additional way to introduce children to poetry.

To introduce children to different kinds of poetry, I hand out construction paper and tell them I will read six poems. The first time they are just to listen and to picture the setting. During the second reading, they are to choose a poem and to begin drawing. My selections are mostly about nature; they are poems by ancient Japanese and Korean poets in the forms of tanka and sijo, forms that predate haiku. They are poems I love. The beauty of the poems slips into the students as easily as their crayons slip across the paper. Students often say to me, "I could just see it in my mind." "I know exactly what the poet means, because that's the way I feel, too." I look at the intensity of their artwork to sense how they have understood the heart of the poem.

And don't overlook poetry as a way to share what your students have learned from a unit of study.

Beluga Whale
White mammal
It swims gracefully
Lives off the coast
Small
by Phoebe

And don't overlook poetry as a way to share what your students have learned from a unit of study. New York City teacher Laura Schwartzberg invites her second-third graders to use poetry to showcase their research. For example, after her students had completed a study of the sea, the children wrote and illustrated sea cinquains. They bound them together to create a beautiful and informational class book. The one way to hook all children on poetry is to

SHOPTALK

Rosen, Michael. *The Best of Michael Rosen.* Berkeley, California: Wetlands Press, 1995.

The London Times said it best: "Michael Rosen is one of those rare people who has never lost touch with what it is like to be ten. He has the rare ability to convey childhood experience in language as simple and intense as the pleasure and pain it describes." Here's a book of poetry to share with your students.It will provoke a range of emotions—and, no doubt, a bevy of poems from your students.

invite poetry teachers into your classroom every day—Karla Kuskin, Aileen Fisher, Jack Preluksky, David McCord—these are some of the marvelous poetry teachers who show us all the poetic possibilities in their own poetry. To write poetry, read poetry.

Parting Thoughts

Endings are important. I wanted to find a good one for this book. I thought about it for a long time, and then I knew it would be best to let others who write daily end the book for me. You know that I love writing. Listen to the voices of teachers and students who love writing, too.

Cynthia Bencal is a sixth-grade teacher in Brookline, Massachusetts. She shares her thoughts about the writing process approach to teaching writing.

> The process approach is not the easiest way to teach writing, but to me it seems the best way. I used to keep much more control over my students' writing and revising when they wrote stories for me. I would guess that over four years' time, I owned about eight hundred stories, from which I leased parts to my students. Some students learned to write better. A few learned to write well. Too few experienced writing as a process for themselves. It is different now. My students own their own stories. They like to write. They are writers now, and best of all they want to continue to be writers when they grow up.

As a case in point, I'll ask six-year-old Kati Lynn Field, a first grader at Yaquina View School in Newport, Oregon, to end the book for us. Kati's principal, Ron Hutchinson, sent me Kati's thoughts on writing. Please see Kati's piece on the next page.

When I grow up I am going to be writer. I'm going to write those big fat books like the ones in the library. People will open those books, and there will be all the words that I wrote for them to read. I like writing a lot. It makes me feel like magic. Sometimes it make me excited, and sometimes it makes me peaceful. I didit learn my writing, I came with it.

Find your writing. Help your students find theirs. Write, learn, and enjoy together.

Professional Bibliography

American Library Association. *Book Links*. Chicago, Illinois: ALA, 1991.

Atwell, Nancie, ed. *Coming To Know: Writing To Learn in the Intermediate Grades*. Portsmouth, New Hampshire: Heinemann, 1990.

———. *In the Middle: Writing, Reading, and Learning with Adolescents*. Portsmouth, New Hampshire: Heinemann, 1987.

Avery, Carol. *...And with a Light Touch: Learning about Reading, Writing, and Teaching with First Graders*. Portsmouth, New Hampshire: Heinemann, 1993.

Bang, Molly. *Wiley and the Hairy Man*. Adapted from an American folktale. New York: Aladdin Books, 1987 [1976].

Barr, Mary. *California Learning Record: Handbook for Teachers, K-6*. Sacramento: California Department of Education, 1993.

Bissex, Glenda L. *GNYS at WRK: A Child Learns To Write and Read*. Cambridge, Massachusetts: Harvard University Press, 1980.

Brady, Sandra. *Let's Make Books*. Dubuque, Iowa: Kendall/Hunt Publishing, 1992.

Bridges, Lois. *Assessment: Continuous Learning*. Strategies for Teaching and Learning Professional Library, The Galef Institute. York, Maine: Stenhouse Publishers, 1995.

————. *Creating Your Classroom Community.* Strategies for Teaching and Learning Professional Library, The Galef Institute. York, Maine: Stenhouse Publishers, 1995.

Bridges Bird, Lois, Kenneth S. Goodman and Yetta M. Goodman. *The Whole Language Catalog: Forms for Authentic Assessment.* Columbus, Ohio: SRA: Macmillan/McGraw Hill, 1994.

Britton, James. *Language and Learning,* 2d ed. Harmondsworth, Middlesex: Penguin, 1993.

Calkins, Lucy McCormick with Shelley Harwayne. *Living between the Lines.* Portsmouth, New Hampshire: Heinemann, 1991.

————. *The Art of Teaching Writing.* New Edition. Portsmouth, New Hampshire: Heinemann, 1994.

————. *Lessons from a Child: On the Teaching and Learning of Writing.* Portsmouth, New Hampshire: Heinemann, 1983.

Chukovskii, Kornei. *From Two to Five.* Translated and edited by Miriam Morton. Berkeley, California: University of California Press, 1968.

Clagget, Fran with Joan Brown. *Drawing Your Own Conclusions: Graphic Strategies for Reading, Writing, and Thinking.* Portsmouth, New Hampshire: Heinemann, 1992.

Collins, Pat. "Bridging the Gap," *Coming To Know,* edited by Nancie Atwell. Portsmouth, New Hampshire: Heinemann, 1990.

Cullinan, Bernice E., Marilyn C. Scala and Virginia C. Schroder. *Three Voices: An Invitation to Poetry across the Curriculum.* York, Maine: Stenhouse Publishers, 1995.

Drew, David. *Caterpillar Diary.* Crystal Lake, Illinois: Rigby Education, 1987.

Duckworth, Eleanor. *The Having of Wonderful Ideas and Other Essays on Teaching and Learning.* New York: Teachers College Press, 1987.

Duthie, Christine. *True Stories: Nonfiction Literacy in the Primary Classroom.* York, Maine: Stenhouse Publishers, 1996.

Dyson, Anne Haas. *Multiple Worlds of Child Writers: Friends Learning To Write.* New York: Teachers College Press, 1989.

Fletcher, Ralph. *What a Writer Needs.* Portsmouth, New Hampshire: Heinemann, 1993.

————. *Walking Trees: Teaching Teachers in the New York City Schools.* Portsmouth, New Hampshire: Heinemann, 1991.

Fox, Mem. *Radical Reflections: Passionate Opinions on Teaching, Learning, and Living.* San Diego: Harcourt Brace & Company, 1993.

Freeman, Evelyn B. and Diane Goetz Person, eds. *Using Nonfiction Trade Books in the Elementary Classroom: From Ants to Zeppelins.* Urbana, Illinois: National Council of Teachers of English, 1992.

Gamberg, Ruth, Winnifred Kwak, Meredith Hutchings and Judy Altheim with Gail Edwards. *Learning and Loving It: Theme Studies in the Classroom.* Portsmouth, New Hampshire: Heinemann, 1988.

Goldberg, Natalie. *Wild Mind: Living the Writer's Life.* New York: Bantam Books, 1990.

———. *Writing Down the Bones: Freeing the Writer Within.* Boston: Shambhala, 1986.

Goodman, Yetta and Bess Attwerger. *"Print Awareness in Preschool Children: A Working Paper"* (Occasional Paper No. 4). Tucson, Arizona: Program in Language and Literary, 1981.

Graves, Donald H. *A Fresh Look at Writing.* Portsmouth, New Hampshire: Heinemann, 1994.

———. *Balance the Basics: Let Them Write.* New York: The Ford Foundation, 1978.

———. *Experiment with Fiction.* Portsmouth, New Hampshire: Heinemann, 1989.

———. *Investigate Nonfiction: The Teacher's Reading and Writing Companion.* Portsmouth, New Hampshire: Heinemann, 1989.

———. *Writing: Teachers and Children at Work.* Portsmouth, New Hampshire: Heinemann, 1983.

Harwayne, Shelley. *Lasting Impressions: Weaving Literature into the Writing Workshop.* Portsmouth, New Hampshire: Heinemann, 1992.

Heard, Georgia. *For the Good of the Earth and Sun: Teaching Poetry.* Portsmouth, New Hampshire: Heinemann, 1989.

Heath, Shirley Brice. "The Functions and Uses of Literacy." *Literacy, Society, and Schooling*, edited by Suzanne de Castell, Alan Luke and Kieran Egan. Cambridge, Massachusetts: Cambridge University Press, 1986.

Heller, Paul G. *Drama as a Way of Knowing.* Strategies for Teaching and Learning Professional Library, The Galef Institute. York, Maine: Stenhouse Publishers, 1995.

Henderson, Kathy. *Market Guide for Young Writers,* 2d ed. Belvidere, New Jersey: Shoe Tree Press, 1988.

Herndon, James. *How To Serve in Your Native Land.* New York: Simon and Schuster, 1971.

Hindley, Joanne. *In the Company of Children.* York, Maine: Stenhouse Publishers, 1996.

Hobart, Ann. *A New Friend for Morganfield: A Story of a Maine Mouse.* Portland, Maine: Gannett Books, 1985.

Kaye, Cathryn Berger. *Word Works: Why the Alphabet Is a Kid's Best Friend.* Boston: Little, Brown and Company, 1985.

Kemper, Dave, Ruth Nathan and Patrick Sebranek. *Writer's Express: A Handbook for Young Writers, Thinkers, and Learners.* Burlington, Wisconsin: Write Source, 1995.

Kitagawa, Mary. "Survey in Language Arts: Writing," *The Whole Language Catalog: Forms for Authentic Assessment,* edited by Lois Bridges Bird, Kenneth S. Goodman and Yetta M. Goodman. Columbus, Ohio: SRA: Macmillan/McGraw Hill, 1994.

Lamott, Anne. *Bird by Bird: Some Instructions on Writing and Life.* New York: Doubleday, 1994.

Learning Media. *Dancing with the Pen: The Learner as Writer.* Wellington, New Zealand: Ministry of Education, 1993.

Lee, Laurie. "I Can't Stay Long," *The Times of Our Lives: A Guide to Writing Autobiography and Memoir,* by Mary Jane Moffat. Santa Barbara, California: John Daniel and Company, 1989.

Lipson, Eden Ross. *The New York Times Parent's Guide to the Best Books for Children.* New York: Times Books, 1988.

MacLachlan, Patricia. *Sarah, Plain and Tall.* New York: Harper & Row, 1985.

Moline, Steve. *I See What You Mean: Children at Work with Visual Information.* York, Maine: Stenhouse Publishers, 1995.

Moll, Luis C., Amarti D. Neff and N. Gonzales. "Funds of Knowledge for Teaching: A Qualitative Approach to Connect Households and Classrooms." *Theory into Practice.* 31(2): 1992.

Mosle, Sara. "Writing Down Secrets," *The New Yorker.* September 18, 1995.

Murray, Donald Morison. *A Writer Teaches Writing: A Practical Method of Teaching Composition.* Boston: Houghton Mifflin, 1968.

O'Dell, Scott. *Island of the Blue Dolphins.* Boston: Houghton Mifflin, 1990. [Originally published by Dell, 1960.]

Ohanian, Susan. *Math as a Way of Knowing.* Strategies for Teaching and Learning Professional Library, The Galef Institute. York, Maine: Stenhouse Publishers, 1995.

Ostrow, Jill. *A Room with a Different View: First Through Third Graders Build Community and Create Curriculum.* York, Maine: Stenhouse Publishers, 1995.

National Council of Teachers of English. *Adventuring with Books: A Booklist for Pre-K–Grade 6.* Urbana, Illinois: NCTE, 1992.

Newman, Judith. *The Craft of Children's Writing*. Portsmouth, New Hampshire: Heinemann, 1984.

Page, Nick. *Music as a Way of Knowing*. Strategies for Teaching and Learning Professional Library, The Galef Institute. York, Maine: Stenhouse Publishers, 1995.

Paterson, Katherine. *Jacob, Have I Loved*. New York: Crowell, 1980.

Rosen, Michael. *The Best of Michael Rosen*. Berkeley, California: Wetlands Press, 1995.

Rosen, Michael and Judith Nicholls. *Count to Five and Say "I'm Alive!"* Poetry Writing Workshops. York, Maine: Stenhouse Publishers, 1995.

Smith, Frank. *Writing and the Writer*. New York: Holt, Rinehart & Winston, 1982.

Steffey, Stephanie and Wendy Hood, eds. *If This Is Social Studies, Why Isn't It Boring?* York, Maine: Stenhouse Publishers, 1994.

Steig, William. *Sylvester and the Magic Pebble*. New York: Windmill/Wanderer Books, 1980. [Originally published by the Trumpet Club, 1969.]

Stott, Jon C. *Children's Literature from A to Z: A Guide for Parents and Teachers*. New York: McGraw-Hill Book Company, 1984.

Strunk, William Jr. and E.B. White. *The Elements of Style*. New York: Macmillan, 1979.

Tannen, Deborah, ed. "Hearing Voices in Conversation, Fiction, and Mixed Genres," *Linguistics in Context: Connecting Observation and Understanding: Lectures from the 1985 LSA/TESOL and NEH Institutes*. Norwood, New Jersey: Ablex Publishing, 1988.

Treetop Publishers. *Bare Books* and *Big Bare Books*. Racine, Wisconsin: Treetop Publishing.

Trelease, Jim. *The Read-Aloud Handbook*. New York: Penguin, 1995.

Ueland, Brenda. *If You Want To Write*, 2d ed. Saint Paul, Minnesota: Gray Wolf Press, 1987.

Vygotsky, Lev. *Mind in Society: The Development of Higher Psychological Processes*. Cambridge, Massachusetts: Harvard University Press, 1978.

Weaver, Constance. *Reading Process to Practice: From Socio-Psycholinguistics to Whole Language*. Portsmouth, New Hampshire: Heinemann, 1988.

Weber, Chris, ed. "Spring." *Treasures 2: Stories and Art by Students in Oregon*. Portland, Oregon: Students' Writing and Art Foundation, 1988.

White, E. B. *Charlotte's Web*. New York: Harper & Row, 1952.

White, Maureen. "Student Writing Survey/Interest Inventory," *The Whole Language Catalog: Forms for Authentic Assessment*, edited by Lois Bridges

Bird, Kenneth S. Goodman and Yetta M. Goodman. Columbus, Ohio: SRA: Macmillan/McGraw Hill, 1994.

Whiteley, Opal. *Opal: The Journal of an Understanding Heart.* New York: Crown Trade Books, 1984. [Originally published by Atlantic Monthly Press, 1920.]

Wilde, Jack. *A Door Opens: Writing in Fifth Grade.* Portsmouth, New Hampshire: Heinemann, 1993.

Wilde, Sandra. *You Kan Red This! Spelling and Punctuation for Whole Language Classrooms, K–6.* Portsmouth, New Hampshire: Heinemann, 1992.

Williams, Margery. *The Velveteen Rabbit.* New York: Avon Books, 1975.

Yashima, Taro. *Umbrella.* New York: Viking Press, 1958.

Zinsser, William Knowlton. *On Writing Well: An Informal Guide to Writing Nonfiction.* New York: Harper and Row, 1985.

Professional Associations and Publications

The American Alliance for Health, Physical Education, Recreation, and Dance (AAHPERD)
Journal of Physical Education, Recreation, and Dance
1900 Association Drive
Reston, Virginia 22091

American Alliance for Theater and Education (AATE)
AATE Newsletter
c/o Arizona State University Theater Department
Box 873411
Tempe, Arizona 85287

American Association for the Advancement of Science (AAAS)
Science Magazine
1333 H Street NW
Washington, DC 20005

American Association of Colleges for Teacher Education (AACTE)
AACTE Briefs
1 DuPont Circle NW, Suite 610
Washington, DC 20036

American Association of School Administrators (AASA)
The School Administrator
1801 North Moore Street
Arlington, Virginia 22209

Association for Childhood Education International (ACEI)
Childhood Education: Infancy Through Early Adolescence
11141 Georgia Avenue, Suite 200
Wheaton, Maryland 20902

Association for Supervision and Curriculum Development (ASCD)
Educational Leadership
1250 North Pitt Street
Alexandria, Virginia 22314

The Council for Exceptional Children (CEC)
Teaching Exceptional Children
1920 Association Drive
Reston, Virginia 22091

Education Theater Association (ETA)
Dramatics
3368 Central Parkway
Cincinnati, Ohio 45225

International Reading Association
(IRA)
The Reading Teacher
800 Barksdale Road
Newark, Delaware 19714

Music Educators National Conference
(MENC)
Music Educators Journal
1806 Robert Fulton Drive
Reston, Virginia 22091

National Art Education Association
(NAEA)
Art Education
1916 Association Drive
Reston, Virginia 22091

National Association for the Education
of Young Children (NAEYC)
Young Children
1509 16th Street NW
Washington, DC 20036

National Association of Elementary
School Principals (NAESP)
Communicator
1615 Duke Street
Alexandria, Virginia 22314

National Center for Restructuring
Education, Schools, and Teaching
(NCREST)
Resources for Restructuring
P.O. Box 110
Teachers College, Columbia University
New York, New York 10027

National Council for the Social Studies
(NCSS)
Social Education
Social Studies and the Young Learner
3501 Newark Street NW
Washington, DC 20016

National Council of Supervisors of
Mathematics (NCSM)
*NCSM Newsletter Leadership in
Mathematics Education*
P.O. Box 10667
Golden, Colorado 80401

National Council of Teachers of
English (NCTE)
Language Arts
Primary Voices K-6
1111 Kenyon Road
Urbana, Illinois 61801

National Council of Teachers of
Mathematics (NCTM)
Arithmetic Teacher
Teaching Children Mathematics
1906 Association Drive
Reston, Virginia 22091

National Dance Association
(NDA)
Spotlight on Dance
1900 Association Drive
Reston, Virginia 22091

National Science Teachers Association
(NSTA)
Science and Children
Science for Children: Resources for Teachers
1840 Wilson Boulevard
Arlington, Virginia 22201

Phi Delta Kappa
Phi Delta Kappan
408 North Union
Bloomington, Indiana 47402

Society for Research in Music Education
Journal for Research in Music Education
c/o Music Educators National Conference
1806 Robert Fulton Drive
Reston, Virginia 22091

The Southern Poverty Law Center
Teaching Tolerance
400 Washington Avenue
Montgomery, Alabama 36104

Teachers of English to Speakers of Other
Languages (TESOL)
TESOL Newsletter
1600 Cameron Street, Suite 300
Alexandria, Virginia 22314

The Strategies for Teaching and Learning Professional Library

Administrators Supporting School Change

Robert Wortman

1-57110-047-4   paperback

Bob Wortman is a talented elementary school principal who writes with conviction and humor of his goals and strategies as a principal in this book directed at all who are interested in school revitalization, especially administrators and curriculum supervisors.

Bob explains the importance of having a vision and philosophy as well as a practical understanding of how people learn, an ability to make use of time and organization, and a concern for maintaining positive relationships with all members of the school community—parents, students, and teachers.

Assessment: Continuous Learning

Lois Bridges

1-57110-048-2   paperback

Effective teaching begins with knowing your students, and assessment is a learning tool that enables you to know them. Indeed, the real power of continuous assessment is that it informs your teaching and helps you decide what to do next.

This book provides a wide range of teacher-developed kidwatching and assessment forms to show different ways to reflect on children's work. It offers developmental checklists, student and child interview suggestions, guidelines for using portfolios, rubrics, and self-evaluation profiles. Also included are *Dialogues* that invite reflection, *Shoptalks* that offer lively reviews of the best and latest professional literature, and *Teacher-To-Teacher Field Notes* offering tips from practicing educators.

Creating Your Classroom **Community**

Lois Bridges

1-57110-049-0   paperback

Chances are the teachers you remember are those who really knew and cared for you as an unique individual with special interests, needs, and experiences. Now, as a teacher with your own classroom and students to care for, you'll want to create a classroom environment that supports each student as an individual while drawing the class together as a thriving learning community.

Creating Your Classroom Community offers the basics of effective elementary school teaching:

- how to create a classroom that supports what we know about learning;
- how to help each of your students to develop and practice self-responsibility;
- how to organize your classroom workspace to best support learning;
- how to construct a curriculum that focuses on your teaching and evaluation methods;
- how to turn to parents and the larger community for classroom support.

Dance as a Way of Knowing
Jennifer Zakkai

1-57110-064-4   paperback

Jennifer Zakkai illuminates how and why dance is a powerful tool for creative learning in K–6 classrooms. Student will learn how to engage in structured learning experiences that demand a high level of concentration and creativity. You don't have to be a dancer to enjoy using the detailed model lessons that take your students through warm-ups, movement explorations, rich curricular integrations, culminating activities, observation, and reflection.

Drama as a Way of Knowing
Paul G. Heller

1-57110-050-4   paperback

You don't have to be a Broadway actor to use drama in your classroom. There's plenty of dramatic energy in your students already, and Paul Heller shows you how to turn it into an effective learning tool.

Through his Ten-Step Process in which you, the teacher, are the director, he shows what you should do to guide your students through rewarding dramatic experiences. You'll find out how to use drama techniques to enable students to access and explore the curriculum in ways that promote deeper thinking. Moving beyond techniques, he also presents the nuts and bolts of pantomime and improvisation, of writing and acting scenes, even creating and presenting large-scale productions.

Literature as a Way of Knowing
Kathy G. Short

1-57110-063-6   paperback

Basal programs cannot provide the variety and choice of reading materials that meet students' needs. Stories that are worth reading and that extend children's experiences and enrich their minds also motivate them to make reading part of their lives. Kathy Short outlines the four roles literature plays in the curriculum and shows you how to use real books to help children learn. She concludes with a discussion of evaluation as part of the curriculum and offers specific examples of evaluation techniques and samples of appropriate forms.

Math as a Way of Knowing

Susan Ohanian

1-57110-051-2   paperback

Award-winning author Susan Ohanian conducts a lively tour of classrooms around the country where "math time" means stimulating learning experiences. To demonstrate that mathematics is an active, ongoing way of perceiving and interacting with the world, she explores teaching mathematical concepts through hands-on activities, writing and talking about what numbers mean, and discovering the where and why of math in everyday life.

Focusing on the NCTM's Standards, Susan takes you into classrooms for a firsthand look at exciting ways the standards are implemented. For the nonspecialist in particular, Susan shows that math really is an exciting and powerful tool that students can readily understand and apply.

Music as a Way of Knowing

Nick Page

1-57110-052-0   paperback

Rich with ideas on how to use music in the classroom, *Music as a Way of Knowing* will appeal especially to classroom teachers who are not musicians, but who enjoy and learn from music and want to use it with their students. Indeed, Nick Page reveals the truth of the adage "If you can talk, you can sing. If you can walk, you can dance."

Nick provides simple instructions for writing songs, using music to support learning across the curriculum, teaching singing effectively, and finding good songs. He assures you that with time, all students can sing well. The good news is that once you've read this book, you'll have the confidence to trust yourself—and your students—to sing and learn well through the joy and power of music.

Second Language Learners

Stephen Cary

1-57110-065-2   paperback

Stephen Cary helps K–5 teachers and administrators bring second language learners at all levels of English language proficiency into the core curriculum. With plenty of charts, visuals, and student samples as text support, Stephen shows you that comprehensible, engaging instruction means SSL kids acquire more content and more language. Whether involved in SLL program planning, coordinating staff-development workshops, or teaching in an elementary classroom, you'll find an abundance of ideas in this book.

Writing as a Way of Knowing

Lois Bridges

1-57110-062-8   paperback

You can help your students become flexible writers who understand all that writing can do and who know how to use it to serve their own purposes.

With Lois Bridges as your guide, you'll explore the many ways to develop young writers:

- how to run a writer's workshop;
- how to implement effective mini-lessons;
- how to conduct thought-provoking writing conferences;
- how to handle revising, editing, and publishing;
- how to recognize the qualities of effective writing.

Lois also explains how to teach the basic skills within the context of real writing, and how to help young writers monitor their own use of conventional spelling, punctuation, and grammar. She covers writing as it applies throughout the curriculum in a chapter on students as independent researchers, tracking down, sorting, and presenting data in a wide variety of formats, and outlines a four-step instructional strategy for introducing new genres, including journal writing and poetry.